on track ...
Iron Maiden

every album, every song

Steve Pilkington

sonicbondpublishing.com

Sonicbond Publishing Limited
www.sonicbondpublishing.co.uk
Email: info@sonicbondpublishing.co.uk

First Published in the United Kingdom 2020
First Published in the United States 2020

British Library Cataloguing in Publication Data:
A Catalogue record for this book is available from the British Library

Copyright Steve Pilkington 2020

ISBN 978-1-78952-061-3

Typeset in ITC Garamond & ITC Avant Garde
Printed and bound in England

Graphic design and typesetting: Full Moon Media

on track ...

Iron Maiden

Contents

Introduction 5

Iron Maiden 8

Killers 17

The Number of the Beast 25

Piece Of Mind 33

Powerslave 43

Somewhere in Time 51

Seventh Son of a Seventh Son 60

No Prayer for the Dying 68

Fear of the Dark 76

The X Factor 83

Virtual XI 91

Brave New World 97

Dance of Death 106

A Matter of Life and Death 116

The Final Frontier 125

The Book of Souls 132

Live Albums, Videos and Compilations 139

Afterword: 30 Numbers of the Beast – Author's Maiden Playlist 142

Bibliography: 142

Acknowledgements

Thanks to Stephen Lambe, for his continuing faith in me by commissioning this book! Will he never learn?

Thanks to Janet, for hearing about Iron Maiden until the words had lost all meaning, and still not complaining.

Thanks to Bryan Cline, for happening to have a camera handy in the US in the early '80s!

Thanks to all the people I hung out with at various rock pubs and clubs back in 1980, when the crucible of the New Wave Of British Heavy Metal forged so much great music. What times.

Thanks to everyone at the *Velvet Thunder* website, in particular fellow Maiden fan Lee Vickers.

Finally, thanks to all of the Maiden guys for inspiration and joy over the years, particularly Bruce Dickinson, the finest heavy metal vocalist of all time (or at least in a death match with Dio) and Janick Gers, who particularly inspired me when I first saw him with White Spirit, who were a magnificent band.

And of course, you who hold this in your hands now. I truly hope you enjoy it!

Up The Irons!

Introduction

The history of Iron Maiden is inextricably bound up with founder member and bassist Steve Harris. A native of Leytonstone, in East London, Harris formed the very first Iron Maiden incarnation on Christmas Day 1975, having previously cut his teeth in bands called Gypsy's Kiss and Smiler. He was 19 at the time. This initial line-up, with Paul Day on vocals, guitarists Terry Rance and Dave Sullivan, and drummer Ron Matthews, didn't last too long. Vocalist Day (who would later front the band More with some success) was replaced in 1976 by Dennis Wilcock, allegedly for his lack of stage presence. This issue was certainly addressed by the recruitment of the flamboyant Wilcock, a Kiss fan who brought blood capsules and face paint to the band's shows!

A good friend of Wilcock was guitarist Dave Murray, who Harris wanted to bring into the band. This met with significant resistance from Rance, however, and to allow the recruitment of Murray to take place, Harris disbanded Maiden in December 1976, only to reform the band shortly afterwards with Murray as the sole guitarist. Things didn't remain stable for too long, however, with the seemingly volatile Wilcock convincing Harris to fire both Matthews and Murray, while a second guitarist named Bob Sawyer was soon ousted after he pretended to play the guitar with his teeth on stage in less than successful fashion, with the audience all fully able to see it was a trick. Down to a duo, Harris now put together a completely new line-up in the second half of 1977, including guitarist Terry Wapram, drummer Barry Purkis (aka Thunderstick, who would go on to play in Samson along with a certain Bruce Dickinson) and keyboard player Tony Moore (later of Cutting Crew). Needless to say, this didn't last long either – especially so in the case of Thunderstick and Moore, who were both ousted after a single gig, Thunderstick having played appallingly and Moore let go as Harris realised the keyboard experiment wasn't working.

Drummer Doug Sampson was brought in to replace Thunderstick, having been in the audience for the outgoing man's only show. After a conversation with an exasperated Harris, he joined that very evening. Things were starting to look a little Spinal Tap on the drummer front, but the next replacements would be in the guitar and vocal roles, with Wilcock deciding to leave having had enough, the firing of the whole band repeatedly seemingly not agreeing with him, and with that departure the door was held open long enough for Murray to immediately be reinstated. The new vocalist was also significant, with Paul Di'Anno coming in to fill the Wilcock shoes, after a chance meeting with Harris in a Leytonstone pub. At this point Murray could be forgiven for getting something of a persecution complex, as Wapram, having only ever been the sole guitarist, objected so strongly to the Murray return that he was himself sacked!

At this point, the band embarked on a guitarist revolving door policy which made their earlier drum stool rotation seem the very model of stability, as guitarist Paul Cairns was brought in to replace Wapram. He lasted three

5

months, leaving in early 1979, after failing to fit in properly by most accounts. Perhaps his nickname of 'Mad Mac' should have rung some alarm bells. His replacement was a man named Paul Todd, who lasted a week before having to leave because, according to Harris, his girlfriend wouldn't let him play live! He was in turn replaced by Tony Parsons, who lasted a few weeks before exiting because, put bluntly, he was not thought to be up to the required standard. Finally, the fourth partner in less than a year for the surely by now paranoid Murray arrived in the shape of Dennis Stratton, and the line-up which would record the band's debut album was finally put in place in December of 1979, when drummer Sampson, who was unable to cope with the band's touring schedule, was replaced by Clive Burr, who was brought into the band at the suggestion of Stratton, on December 26 – four years and a day (and sixteen band members!) since Harris assembled the first line-up.

After the release of the debut album, and prestigious support tours with Kiss and Judas Priest, Stratton was dismissed with 'personal and creative differences' being cited, and he was replaced by Murray's childhood friend Adrian Smith. Smith had been asked to join a year earlier, but he declined because of his commitment to his band Urchin, and Stratton was hired instead. The partnership of Murray and Smith would remain intact for the next decade, but the single most significant personnel change of the band's career was waiting in the wings.

After the release of the second album, *Killers*, in 1981, Paul Di'Anno, who had become steadily more unreliable following increased alcohol and drug use, was fired from the band to the shock and bemusement of much of the band's fanbase. A large part of the band's 'punky', 'New Wave of British Heavy Metal' attitude had been embodied by Di'Anno's leather jacket and short hair image, and the stark choice was whether to go for a like-for-like replacement or try to open up the band's appeal to a wider audience. They went for the latter, with the recruitment of Bruce Dickinson, the man who personifies Maiden, along with Harris, in the public's perception of the band.

Dickinson had been fronting the band Samson (which included Thunderstick at the time) under the stage name of Bruce Bruce (a nickname derived from the *Monty Python* 'Bruces' sketch) and had recorded two albums with them. He first encountered Maiden when they actually supported Samson at a gig at the Music Machine in London in 1980, and right from that moment knew he wanted to join them. When that offer came, a year later, he needed little persuasion, and the band almost immediately changed. Gone were the short, sharp songs about life on the streets, such as 'Running Free' and 'Sanctuary', being replaced by a much greater concentration on highly literate, story-telling lyrics and a more mature, progressive element to the band's sound. Dickinson's on-stage appearance with long hair and a voice dubbed the 'air raid siren' cemented this change and led to an immediate career jump with *The Number of the Beast* album. There would be one further line-up change, with the increasingly erratic Burr being replaced on drums by Nicko McBrain after the tour to promote the record (once again, this meeting had come about through a show together, when McBrain's band Trust supported Maiden) but this line-up would then remain in place throughout the 1980s.

The next change occurred in 1990 when Adrian Smith left the band during work on the album *No Prayer for the Dying*, after musical differences with Harris, and he was replaced by Janick Gers, formerly with White Spirit and Gillan. Following one further album, Dickinson himself dropped the bombshell of leaving in 1993, to concentrate on a solo career, and the band had their first real crisis in a long time. Blaze Bayley, from the band Wolfsbane, was brought in to replace him, which was only partially successful, and after two more albums, he was dismissed in 1999. At this point, while replacement singers were being considered, the band's manager Rod Smallwood persuaded Harris that they should approach Dickinson about coming back. After some deliberation, this was done, and the pair buried the hatchet, to the delight of fans. To add to this, Adrian Smith also returned and, with Gers being retained, the band now had a three-guitar six-piece line-up which continues to this day.

Iron Maiden

Personnel:
Paul Di'Anno: vocals
Dave Murray: guitars
Dennis Stratton: guitars
Steve Harris: bass guitar
Clive Burr: drums
Record Label: EMI (UK), Harvest/Capitol (US)
Recorded: January 1980, produced by Will Malone
UK release date: 14 April 1980. US release date: August 1980
Highest chart places: UK: 4, USA: Did not chart
Running time: 37:35

The seeds of this album date back to the final two days of 1978, when the band as it was (including Sampson on drums and an uncredited Paul Cairns on guitar) spent two days recording a four-track demo tape at Spaceward Studios in Cambridge. The songs in question were 'Prowler', 'Iron Maiden', 'Invasion' and 'Strange World'. Due to the master tapes being wiped, the band were unable to record some overdubs as they planned and were left with those rough recordings. Early in 1979, Steve Harris gave a copy of the tape to Neal Kay, the influential metal DJ at the 'Bandwagon Soundhouse' venue in North London, and he began playing it regularly. With the songs (particularly 'Prowler') featuring in the 'Soundhouse Heavy Metal Chart' published in *Sounds*, fans started asking for the material to be made available. Accordingly, in November 1979, 5000 copies were pressed up and released on the band's own Rock Hard label as *The Soundhouse Tapes*, featuring three tracks ('Strange World' was considered not to be of good enough quality). The red cover featured a photo of a shirtless Di'Anno on stage, with notes written by Neal Kay on the reverse. Original copies of this are now a sought after collectors' item.

A month after the release of the EP, and no doubt largely on the back of the demand for it, the band signed a recording contract with EMI, and almost immediately went into the studio to begin work on their first album. Recorded in January 1980, the album was produced by Will Malone, who had arranged the strings (as The Flux Fiddlers) on Black Sabbath's landmark album *Sabbath Bloody Sabbath*. The union was not entirely successful, however, with Harris later claiming that Malone had little interest in the project and that the band were largely left to finish it off themselves over the course of two weeks. Various band members have often been quoted as saying that they regarded the production as lifeless and generally substandard. However, a vocal minority of fans loudly proclaim it as being the perfect distillation of the band's raw and dirty incarnation at that time.

The album appeared in April of 1980, but two months before this (after recording was completed but before the release) two Iron Maiden tracks appeared on the album *Metal for Muthas*, which was compiled by Neal Kay and featured a selection of the New Wave of British Heavy Metal (generally known as NWOBHM) bands. The two Maiden tracks, versions of 'Sanctuary' and 'Wrathchild', were, in fact, demo versions recorded as a four-piece shortly before Stratton's arrival, and featured Sampson on drums. The album reached Number 12 on the UK album charts – a great showing for a compilation of this type – and therefore these two demos became very heavily listened to by fans.

Album Cover:

The album cover art is by the man who would become the band's long-time regular artist, Derek Riggs. It features an early (and rather rudimentary) rendition of the band's mascot, 'Eddie' (named from the fact that the mask which was the original Eddie was known as 'The Head', which in the band's East London accent became 'The 'Ead'). On the album cover, he is standing in front of a wall at night, with street lamps and an overflowing litter bin in the background. Eddie had made his first appearance in February on the cover of the single 'Running Free', where he is seen standing in the shadows holding a broken bottle. His face is obscured by the shadow because the band wanted his full appearance to be saved for the album – somewhat of an anti-climax if we are honest, as he does look somewhat 'gormless' as opposed to menacing! The covers of contemporary singles by the band had arguably better artwork in fact: 'Running Free' had a long-haired youth running through an alley with Eddie looming behind (the names of bands such as Scorpions, Led Zep, AC/DC and Judas Priest can be seen as graffiti, along with 'Hammers', representing Harris's beloved West Ham United football team), 'Sanctuary' sees him standing over a prone Margaret Thatcher, knife in hand, while 'Women in Uniform' depicts Thatcher as miraculously reborn, and lying in wait in military garb as Eddie strolls past with a nurse and a schoolgirl!

Riggs used to incorporate a small version of his own logo in all of his cover art, and on the *Iron Maiden* album cover, it can be seen on a brick in the wall just to the left of Eddie. On the cover of 'Running Free' it is on a box, on the cover of the 'Sanctuary' single it is on a poster peeling off a wall and on 'Women in Uniform' it is just below Margaret Thatcher's elbow.

'Prowler' (Harris)

Opening with a strident, wah-wah-driven guitar riff, this is a great way for Maiden to kick off their album debut. After the first appearances of that riff, the band kick straight into high gear and a propulsive, irresistible tempo. The riff reappears after the first verse and chorus, this time riding the thunder of the whole band, and it's glorious. Things get a little confused after this point, however, with an awkward break and a slightly clumsy sounding riff appearing just at the point when the momentum is at full pace. The energy thus built up is dissipated slightly here, though things are soon back on track with Murray's fluid and exciting solo. All is forgiven as that great wah-wah figure reappears to whirl the listener away to the song's climax. This is early Iron Maiden in a

9

nutshell.

Lyrically, the track is rather undemanding, telling as it does the insalubrious tale of a 'flasher' at large, 'crawling through the bushes' and 'feeling myself', but it does fit the raw, untamed feel of the music to a tee. The earlier version on *The Soundhouse Tapes* is rawer still, with much more of a 'live' feel to it, and for sheer energy and breathless excitement it may even be said to surpass the album version. Certainly, the band (and Di'Anno, it must be said) sound lean, hungry and playing as if their very lives are at stake.

'Remember Tomorrow' (Harris, Di'Anno)

For those who still swear that Maiden was a better band with Di'Anno, this astonishing song is, without doubt, one of their strongest arguments. A slow tempo ballad with crushingly heavy sections, the song does certainly contain more than the occasional echo of 'Beyond the Realms of Death' by Judas Priest but creates its own strong identity for all of that. Di'Anno pours real soul into his vocal, and the way he soars into the word 'sky' at the end of the second verse recalls Rob Halford at his absolute best. The first guitar solo is by Dave Murray, while the second, from around 3:08, is Stratton.

The lyrics are beautifully oblique, with no clear meaning yet always hinting at something profound which is just out of reach. Di'Anno, who wrote the words, has said on more than one occasion that it was inspired by his grandfather. In an interview with journalist Greg Prato, he explained that his grandfather died from complications arising from diabetes in 1980, and that 'Remember Tomorrow' was a 'catch-phrase' of his, claiming that he used to say 'Remember tomorrow – it might be a better day'. It has been widely claimed that Di'Anno's grandfather was, in fact, a pilot during the Second World War and that the imagery in the lyrics comes directly from that, but while it does fit the interpretation, there is no hard evidence to support the theory.

'Running Free' (Harris, Di'Anno)

From the sublime to the... well, different. This song, the first single released by the band, also has a Di'Anno lyric but has absolutely none of the atmosphere, subtlety or soul of 'Remember Tomorrow'. Which is not necessarily a criticism, it is simply a very different type of song. The lyrical content in this one is clear for all to see, as it eulogises the teenage pleasures of being a rebel and 'running free', with no responsibilities. Musically, it is very simple, with the drumbeat anchoring the whole thing to a very repetitive, yet catchy, verse-chorus structure. Harris and Di'Anno have both claimed to have come up with the musical idea, with Harris claiming he wrote the riff around Doug Sampson's drum part in the first place, while Di'Anno claims to have taken the almost tribal drumbeat from the single 'Rock and Roll, Parts One and Two' by the now-disgraced Gary Glitter.

Whatever the truth of the matter, it is a song which does its job and does it well enough, without ever claiming to be great art. The instrumental section of the track is unusual as, instead of a solo, there is a sort of call-and-response between Harris's bass lines and quickfire guitar fills. In fact, early versions of the song had a Murray guitar solo included, but this was dropped before the final recording.

As an aside, listening to the power chords in the song's intro gives a definite feeling of Black Sabbath's 'Children of the Grave'. It is undeniably true that at this point Maiden – and largely Harris, of course – wore their influences proudly on their sleeves, as with the Judas Priest echoes in the previous track. Rather than originality, the Maiden *modus operandi* at this point in their career was one of taking the influences they loved and forging them into their own vision, and one has to say they did it pretty well.

Note: when Maiden was invited onto the BBC's *Top of the Pops* to perform the song, they refused to lip-synch to a backing track, which was the norm, and insisted that they would only perform if they could play live. This made them the first band to do so since The Who, some six years earlier.

'Phantom of the Opera' (Harris)

Probably the most enduring and celebrated track on the debut in terms of audience popularity, 'Phantom of the Opera' marks the first indication of Steve Harris' prog-rock leanings and love of literary and historical lyrical influences. In this case, of course, the song is inspired by the 1910 novel by Gaston Leroux, since filmed several times and also turned into the famous musical by Andrew LloydWebber. It is clear, however, that Harris does not want to steer the ship too far into proggy waters just yet, as, despite its seven-minute duration and numerous twists and turns along the way, the riff is still king, and the lyric is relatively brief at only sixteen lines.

The intro to the song is utterly iconic, with the band kicking into a galloping riff as Di'Anno shouts 'Oh yeah!'. This part of the track never gets old, and indeed displayed its innate sense of momentum and energy when it was later used in a TV advert for Lucozade, kicking into gear just as athlete Daley Thompson left the starting blocks – a perfect combination of music and visuals. After a couple of initial verses, there is a break into an instrumental section going through transitions from slow to fast and heavy, with the first two solos (one slow, one fast) taken by Murray and the third by Stratton, before the first part of the song reasserts itself for the coda. Following a short break at the end, after a sudden climax, Di'Anno's voice suddenly returns, heavily distorted, repeating the line 'you torture me back at your lair'.

As excellent as the song is, it isn't perfect. The band's songwriting skills were still evolving at this point, and there are examples of that here (as in parts of 'Prowler', for example), where it tries to get a little too complex and slightly overreaches the band's abilities at the time. When Di'Anno first comes in, the lines have so many words crammed in that he has to uncomfortably babble them as fast as he can, to the point of being almost indecipherable, with the fact that he is doubling the guitar melody making this feel a little clumsy, and some of the changes in the instrumental section are too stark, with no feeling of flowing naturally. Nevertheless, this was still an impressive achievement for this early time in the band's career, and it has gone on to be very effective on stage. Harris's bass is especially effective and well used in the piece.

'Transylvania' (Harris)

Unusually for Iron Maiden, this Side Two opener is an instrumental (they only ever recorded four – though two of the other three are on the following album *Killers*, with only one after Dickinson joined. Make of that what you will). In fact, 'Transylvania' was originally intended to have lyrics, with the vocal melody line written, but the band decided it sounded so good as it was that writing a lyric for the sake of it would be pointless.

This was a good decision, as the track stands on its own as truly excellent. After a short intro, a galloping moderately fast section kicks off with the dual lead guitars of Murray and Stratton combining on a theme rather reminiscent of Thin Lizzy's classic 'Emerald' – and none the worse for that. After a couple of minutes, the tempo kicks up to double time, and in an almost 'Freebird'-esque conclusion, the guitarists solo over this stampeding, heavy backing for the remainder of the track, Stratton on this occasion taking the first solo.

The title is something of a mystery, as there is nothing innate in the sound of the piece to suggest creepy vampiric activity, and indeed, if anything, that first section conjures up more of a Celtic air than anything else. Maybe the lyrics had already been planned to reference vampires (Transylvania, situated in modern-day Romania was, of course, the setting for Bram Stoker's *Dracula*, and has remained synonymous with the undead in public perception). On the other hand, perhaps Steve Harris simply fancied backpacking around Eastern Europe if he got the time! Whatever the truth, the band have not expanded upon it – to the best of my knowledge.

'Strange World' (Harris)

If there is one song which divides fans, it is this one. Slow and dreamlike, it bears some comparisons with 'Remember Tomorrow', but without the heavy sections which still anchor that track to the metal world. In fact, 'Strange World' is a masterful song, all but forgotten by all but the diehard fans. At this time it was actually a live favourite, and the band did record it for the demo tape which became *The Soundhouse Tapes*, though they dropped it, feeling the production was poor.

The guitars carry this song beautifully, with subtle and evocative use of harmonics, and the two solos are magnificent (Stratton taking the opening one this time out). Lyrically it is very obtuse, and open to a wealth of interpretations, but primarily it talks about the issues of living in the real world, and the strange delights of the protagonist's 'new strange world', where you never grow old, girls drink 'plasma wine' and cries are left unheard. This strange world could refer to getting high, or retreating into one's mind to escape the real world, or it may even point to the central character committing suicide and the 'strange world' being the afterlife. It has even been claimed that the segue from 'Transylvania' into this song indicates a vampiric lyrical theme, with lines such as the girls drinking plasma wine pointing to the act of drinking blood, but this is somewhat tenuous, and the fact that 'Transylvania' was originally intended to have its own lyrics makes it still more unlikely.

Whatever the interpretation, this is one of the strongest moments of the whole Di'Anno era, and one which Harris has hinted may be revived on stage at some point. He has commented that Stratton tended to prefer this sort of material over the more direct metal songs, and also that Murray loved playing the solo at live shows, and it would make a fascinating 'deep cut' to unearth. Interestingly, when the band brought back much of the material from the first four albums for the 'Eddie Rips Up the World' tour in 2005, 'Transylvania' and 'Strange World' were the only songs from this album not featured.

'Charlotte the Harlot' (Murray)

Back to rather more prosaic lyrical concerns here with this tale of a London 'working girl', in a song penned solely by Dave Murray – his only solo writing credit with the band. It's very much 'business as usual' musically as well, as the first part of the song clatters by riding a fast, punky riff and a hugely catchy chorus, but at around 1:40 there is an unexpected change. From the lusty descriptions of Charlotte's lifestyle and inimitable charms, suddenly the music breaks down to a slow, reflective passage as the lyric turns to the singer reminiscing about the love he had for Charlotte and how it was shattered. It's an unexpected and surprisingly affecting interlude, before the band come in again and Murray followed by Stratton take two extremely quick guitar solos of around ten seconds each! From this, it's back to the *donner und blitzen* of the first part of the song again, and it is, appropriately, 'wham, bam, thank you ma'am' up to the end. It's very formative Maiden, of course (like much of the album), but it's rather good for all that.

The question as to who Charlotte was, if indeed she was based on a real person, has been asked many times, but a clear answer has never been forthcoming. The one exception to that was a few years ago in an interview with the metal website *Battle Helm*, when Di'Anno suddenly turned all 'supergrass' and delivered an explanation saying that she was a Walthamstow 'legend' named High Hill Lil, complete with the street she lived on. However, it may be that too much credence should not necessarily be placed on this. The singer has been well known over the years for 'embroidering' stories somewhat, and this does seem a lot of information rather, after decades of silence on the matter. There was a follow-up of sorts to this song in the shape of '22 Acacia Avenue' on *The Number Of The Beast* in a couple of years, and 'Charlotte' itself had one more turn in the spotlight as it was re-recorded for a B-side some eight years later.

Trivia fact: 'Charlotte the Harlot' was the name of an American B-26 Marauder aeroplane flown in the Second World War, by a pilot with the unlikely name of First Lieutenant Basil B. 'Bumstead' Burnstad, 319th Bombardier Group, US Air Force. The name, with an accompanying graphic, was painted on the side in a similar fashion to the famous 'Memphis Belle', so it may be that Murray had seen this and took the name from it. Charlotte, sadly, was downed over Italy in 1943, hit by flak.

'Iron Maiden' (Harris)

The band's signature song, and played at the end of every Maiden show since it was first released. It is unquestionably iconic, and one of the most recognisable Maiden tracks to this day, but is it as good as its hallmark reputation would suggest?

The answer to the question is, in purely musical and lyrical terms, probably not. It certainly starts well, with a tremendous guitar riff opening proceedings, and a lightning-fast (and catchy) chorus and verse, but after a minute or so there isn't really a lot more going on. The same verse and chorus are repeated three times in exactly the same way, and the only contrast offered over the three-and-a-half minutes is a short instrumental break around the two-minute mark. Essentially, it's just a bit too repetitive, and when the band come in after the introductory guitar riff, Burr sounds rather leaden behind the kit.

It's a great live song. It's a great 'signature' song. It's a great riff, come to that, but it isn't quite a great song in itself. It closes the album in exciting fashion, though, so it does its job there.

Related songs:

'Sanctuary' (Harris, Di'Anno, Murray)

Originally a non-album single in the UK, 'Sanctuary' was added to the tracklisting when the album was released in the US. The reason for it being omitted from the UK album is claimed to be because an earlier recording of it was released on the compilation album *Metal for Muthas* (which also included 'Wrathchild', which was held over to the second album, for presumably the same reason. The compilation was on the same EMI label as the UK album, so if this is the case it rather appears to be a case of the label restricting themselves! There is also some question over the actual writers of the song; the original single release credits it to the band collectively, though there have been strong claims that it was actually written by guitarist Rob D'Angelo in 1977, and that he was paid to relinquish the credit. From 1998 onward, when it appeared on the UK CD version of the album, the song has been credited to Harris, Di'Anno and Murray.

Whatever the story behind the track, it is a serviceable, if somewhat untaxing romp, in much the same way as the first single 'Running Free'. The band are tight and aggressive, and the riff is razor-sharp, but there is a feeling of energy over substance. The *Metal for Muthas* version was recorded as a four-piece, with Doug Sampson on drums, just before Stratton's arrival, and is a curious beast, in a way. It is certainly less polished than the later single recording and rawer, but there is a punch to it that the rather sterile production job, credited to Malone, lacks. It's quite hard to say which is the better version. Stratton and Murray (in that order) trade solos, whereas Murray is the sole guitarist on the earlier version, but there isn't much to put between the two recordings on that basis.

The B-side of the single contained two live tracks on the 12-inch single version, one a version of 'Drifter', which would appear in studio form on the next album (featuring here a rather unconvincing audience participation section) and which was the sole 7-inch flip side. The other was a cover of the Montrose song 'I've Got the Fire', with Di'Anno clearly struggling with his voice. A studio rendition of this latter track would appear in superior form in 1983 as the B-side of the single 'Flight of Icarus'.

The notorious single artwork, depicting Eddie standing over the body of Margaret Thatcher with a knife, was explained by artist Derek Riggs as being a reference to the fact that Thatcher had been dubbed the Iron Maiden in some quarters after her tough stance with the USSR, with Eddie taking offence to this. She has apparently been ripping down a Maiden poster when he takes his revenge! It's all very tongue in cheek but also done with an eye on baiting the media and getting some press, which worked like a charm.

'Burning Ambition' (Harris)

The B-side to the 'Running Free' single, this is another track which was recorded as a four-piece with Sampson on drums (and the only one officially released apart from the two tracks on *Metal for Muthas*). It was written by Harris back in his pre-Maiden days with Gypsy's Kiss, and sounds almost nothing like Maiden! A light, upbeat and cheery sounding song with some delightfully uplifting double-tracked guitar from Murray, it bears more of a resemblance to early Rush with a little Wishbone Ash thrown in than it does to Maiden circa 1980. A rather nice curio, and a refreshing change, it is a shame it was not better known – though it did eventually see a CD release on the album *Best of the 'B' Sides*, part of the *Eddie's Archive* box set, in 2002.

'Women in Uniform' (Macainsh)

The band's third and last single release with Dennis Stratton in the line-up, and one which they would rather be forgotten. The song is a cover of a track by Australian band Skyhooks, which they were persuaded to do by their publishing company. Harris was unsure about the idea but relented when AC/DC producer Tony Platt was hired. This backfired spectacularly when Platt (with the aid of Stratton) was found to be remixing the band's heavy arrangement to make it sound much more commercial. The preferred mix was restored, but Harris was furious, and Platt was fired on the spot. It can't have strengthened Stratton's position either.

It's perhaps better than the band's relentlessly negative opinion of it, but in truth, it is a poor fit for Maiden, despite its catchy quality. An official promo video shows the band performing the song at The Rainbow Theatre in London, with Di'Anno trying manfully to look convincing and Harris just appearing embarrassed. It was disowned by the band and has rarely appeared on CD. It is notable as one of only four songs in the entire Maiden catalogue to fade out (the others being 'Stranger in a Strange Land', 'The Prophecy' and their cover of Golden Earring's 'Kill Me (Ce Soir)'). The B-side was 'Invasion', discussed below.

The single cover art saw Riggs continuing the theme from 'Sanctuary', with an armed Thatcher waiting around a corner to exact revenge on Eddie who is with, yes, two women in uniform.

'Invasion' (Harris)
An early Harris composition about a Viking invasion, this is much more up the Maiden alley than its A-side 'Women in Uniform', but it is still unremarkable. In truth, this recording sounds somewhat weak in comparison to the original recording on *The Soundhouse Tapes*, which is taken at a slower tempo but possesses more power. The chorus ('The Norsemen are coming, the Norsemen are coming...') is a far cry from the big roof-raising choruses that Maiden would become known for, and it is easy to understand why the track did not make the debut album. It was reworked later as the song 'Invaders' on *The Number of the Beast* and was certainly an improvement.

Killers

Personnel:
Paul Di'Anno: vocals
Dave Murray: guitars
Adrian Smith: guitars
Steve Harris: bass guitar
Clive Burr: drums
Record Label: EMI (UK), Harvest/Capitol (US)
Recorded: Nov 1980 – Jan 1981, produced by Martin Birch
UK release date: 2 Feb 1981. US release date: 6 June 1981
Highest chart places: UK: 12, USA: 78
Running time: 38:18

Following the release of the debut album, a rift had begun to grow between Dennis Stratton and the rest of the band, particularly Harris, who has commented on the fact that he seemed more keen on the lighter, more introspective material, such as 'Strange World' and 'Remember Tomorrow'. In fact, during the recording of the album Stratton was discovered putting multi-layered guitars and Queen-esque backing vocals onto 'Phantom of the Opera', which were immediately removed. With his similar assistance in the tweaking of the 'Women in Uniform' recording, it was clear that things were not going to work, and he was dismissed following the tour in support of the album, in October 1980. Meanwhile, Adrian Smith, who had turned the band down out of loyalty to his own band Urchin, was regretting that decision after Urchin themselves split up early in 1980. After a chance meeting with Harris and Murray, he was asked to reconsider and, after a successful audition, joined the band in November 1980, just a month after Stratton's departure.

One thing the band were adamant about, was that the production must be much better this time, after the Malone debacle. This was all but assured when the services of Martin Birch were secured. Birch, who had cut his engineering and production teeth with Deep Purple during a long association, went on to enjoy a similar lengthy relationship with Maiden, lasting until his retirement in 1992. Most of the songs which would end up on *Killers* had already been written before the debut, with only 'Murders in the Rue Morgue' and 'Prodigal Son' composed specially for the album. None of the tracks had previously been recorded, however, with the sole exception of 'Wrathchild', which featured in demo form on *Metal for Muthas*. The album was recorded at Battery Studios, London, between November 1980 and January 1981.

Album Cover:

Another Derek Riggs cover, of course, this time featuring Eddie, dripping axe in hand, pictured seemingly in mid-attack in front of some urban buildings, which appear to be flats. Eddie looks far more like the finished article this time out, compared to the lobotomised scarecrow which he resembled on the first album: Riggs had his hand in with the character now! The back cover of the album depicted a dramatic photo of the band onstage, all lights and pyrotechnics, with band photos and credits beneath. Interestingly, there is also a photo of Martin Birch, who is credited as 'Martin "Headmaster" Birch', in contrast to his days with Deep Purple when he was known by the nickname 'The Wasp'.

The Riggs logo on the album can be seen in one of the windows in the building to the right of Eddie. The two singles released at the time also had Riggs artwork, with the non-album single 'Twilight Zone' featuring a young woman (Eddie's lover from the song's lyric) sitting at a dressing table as his ghost looms behind her, while the follow-up 'Purgatory' showed a devil's face decaying to reveal Eddie beneath. Interestingly, the original artwork for 'Purgatory' was what became the cover of the band's next album *Number of the Beast* – they held it back as it was felt to be so good, and Riggs had to hastily come up with the replacement art for the single. The Riggs logo is carved into the nightstand on 'Twilight Zone' and is just beside the devil's face on 'Purgatory'.

'The Ides of March' (Harris)
At only a minute and 44 seconds, this instrumental is the shortest track ever recorded by Iron Maiden. It has been remarked upon many times that this is essentially the same track as 'Thunderburst' by Samson, included on their album *Head On*, released in 1980 and the first of their albums to feature Bruce Dickinson. The simple reason for this is that the track was written by Harris with Samson drummer Thunderstick during the short time he was a member of Maiden. Both elected to use it for their respective bands – though oddly, while the Samson version is credited to both of them, Harris claims sole credit for this version.

In fact, it is an effective and dramatic album opener, driven by a hypnotic and almost tribal drum pattern, which can probably be assumed to be Thunderstick's contribution. At around 40 seconds Adrian Smith comes in with his first Maiden guitar solo, followed by Murray taking over at the minute mark. The Samson track loses out by not having this strong guitar work, but it is possibly more strident and powerful in its sound, so the two versions both have their merits. 'Thunderburst' has an acoustic intro not used on 'The Ides of March', but with the drum backbone still present, losing the Thunderstick credit seems strange.

The title, of course, comes from the name given to the 15th of March in Roman times, and the date on which Julius Caesar is said to have been murdered – making this an early example of Steve Harris's love of historical references. On the subsequent tour, this was played as the intro music, with the band immediately going into 'Wrathchild', in exactly the same way as it does on the album...

'Wrathchild' (Harris)

Probably the most celebrated and enduring song from *Killers*, and with good reason, 'Wrathchild' follows on from 'The Ides of March' seamlessly, the lyrics telling of the vengeful protagonist hunting down the father who abandoned him. Right from the bass-driven opening, courtesy of Harris, this is 'old school' metal with its flag proudly flying, owing far more to Mk.III Deep Purple and *Rising*-period Rainbow than the punkier moments of the debut, settling into a loping groove and remorselessly pursuing it. There are notable differences between this and the earlier *Metal for Muthas* take of the song, most notably that this is taken at a faster pace with Smith weaving guitar embellishments over the riff which were not present previously. The *Killers* recording is, without doubt, tighter and more polished, but the earlier version does have a certain raw power, deriving from the slightly slower tempo. The central riff bears a significant resemblance to Deep Purple's 'Stormbringer' (never a bad thing), which is far more obvious on that first recording.

With this opening one-two, Maiden made it quite clear to anyone listening that they had upped their game from spirited rockers full of youthful energy, to a serious metal force, and Martin Birch must take great credit for that.

'Murders in the Rue Morgue' (Harris)

At first glance, this would appear to be a song retelling the Edgar Allan Poe story of the same name, but actually the two are only loosely connected. They both begin with killings in the aforementioned Parisian street, but whereas the Poe story is very much a detective story unravelling the (surprising) identity of the killer, the song takes the murder of two women overheard by the central character as the springboard for him being mistakenly accused of the crime and pursued throughout France. Interestingly, this rather simplistic tale is given a little twist in the tale in the last line when he worries that his doctor has told him he's 'done it before', raising the possibility that he may have schizophrenia, not realising that he is indeed the perpetrator. A nice wrinkle for sure, though there are some clumsy lyrics here, such as the dreadfully awkward 'I can't speak French, so I couldn't explain'. Harris was an ambitious songwriter, but still honing his craft.

Musically, at slightly over four minutes, the song is almost as schizophrenic as its perpetrator hints at being, with the first minute or so effectively being like a different track. What a minute, though, as the delicate guitar and bass intro leads to 30 seconds of glorious progressive-influenced anthemic riffing, all strident guitars and soaring lead lines. Listen out for Harris playing harmonics on the bass at the beginning here, incidentally. He has said that he had never tried that particular technique very much before, but that it was an experiment in creating the mood, which it does brilliantly. At around a minute in, however, things change on a dime as the band crash in with a powerful and fun, though comparatively simplistic fast-paced rocker, sung well by Di'Anno, and capturing the thrill of the chase as he outruns the law.

However, this section undeniably leaves a sense of what might have been, had they developed that first minute across the whole song. There's a nice guitar solo, however, with Smith and Murray combining on a twin-guitar effort which gives the song a very effective mid-section.

Just don't expect a scholarly reinvention of the Poe tale. A good song it is, but 'The Rime of the Ancient Mariner' it is not!

'Another Life' (Harris)
An enjoyable enough song this one, but most would probably agree it is not the album's strongest contribution. It starts off very powerfully, with Murray opening up with some blistering fretwork before the vocals come in. Here is where things go a little awry, however, as Harris follows up the first verse about a man feeling hopeless and contemplating suicide by inexplicably simply delivering exactly the same lines three times – just as in the earlier 'Iron Maiden' song itself. It's doubly frustrating on this occasion, however, as what lyrics there are, paint an intriguing scenario, but we never get to find out whether our unfortunate depressive is redeemed or goes through with it, simply hearing him talking about it three times. Perhaps he was depressed because he was living through Groundhog Day, who knows...

Musically, we're in fast-paced, quite catchy but unmemorable territory, though Murray's guitar work, and his solo in mid-song, certainly does its best to lift it to a higher level. It's nice to listen to, but you might struggle to recall it after the album finishes.

'Genghis Khan' (Harris)
Another instrumental track, though longer and more complex this time. Once again, according to Harris, there were plans to add a vocal. However, as with 'Transylvania', they felt it was too good as it was to change it. The track goes through various tempo changes, managing to conjure up the image of Genghis Khan's armies going into battle pretty successfully. Harris has said that he deliberately chose not to have any guitar solos in the track, and on this occasion, it is a shrewd move, as the chaotic, claustrophobic 'battle' aura of the music might well be diluted by a guitar leaving the dense 'sonic soup' to deliver a solo.

Over the years there has been much controversy surrounding the riff at around 1:48 and its close similarity to the massive selling song 'Last Resort' by nu-metallers Papa Roach. They have denied any deliberate lift, but let us just say that the similarity is somewhat striking! Nicko McBrain has said that the song was written quickly to fill up some space left on the record and that the working title was 'Jenkins Barn', but since he was still two albums away from joining the band, this may or may not be reliable. He is certainly a man who enjoys a joke, without any doubt, but it is interesting if true.

'Innocent Exile' (Harris)
This track, closing the original first side of vinyl, could be construed as a

companion piece of sorts to 'Rue Morgue', as the lyrics concern the plight of a fugitive from justice, bemoaning the hopelessness of his situation and claiming that he wasn't responsible for the murder of which he is accused. The circumstances of the offence make it conceivable that it could be intended to be the same individual.

Leaving that aside, this is another song of two halves, as it were. The first couple of minutes have Di'Anno singing in an unusually gruff voice, sounding almost like David Coverdale at times, and indeed the riff added to the voice give it a slight feel of Mk.III Deep Purple crossed with one of Black Sabbath's sprightlier moments. After that point, the tempo kicks up again, and the instrumental coda features two blistering guitar solos, with Murray leading off for Smith to follow.

According to Harris, the opening bass riff went through some changes as the song developed. He wrote it on bass for guitar, and it was first played on the guitar with the bass playing a sort of power chord backing to it, but in the end, they reversed it again, the riff itself returned to the bass, and the guitars reverted to providing the slashing chordal accompaniment.

'Killers' (Harris, Di'Anno)

Another song concerning a killer, but in this case, there is no pretence of innocence, only the unnerving delight of the perpetrator reliving the excitement and the rush of the murder. This is a look into the mind of a serial killer, nothing more or less, and to Di'Anno's credit, he gets inside the lyric superbly. Interestingly, this is his only writing contribution to the album, whereas he wrote several sets of lyrics on the debut.

The opening riff is once again very bass-dominated, as Harris continues to make his presence felt strongly on the album. It takes around a minute of riffery accompanied by demented screams from Di'Anno – really warming to his task – before the tempo is upped again and away we go onto the song proper. The riff, over which the verses are sung, is an interestingly stop-start affair, with a charging run followed by a break at the end of each line, in a similar way to 'Barracuda' by Heart. It works well in allowing the song, and Di'Anno's portrayal, to 'breathe', in a way that, say, 'Phantom of the Opera', for all its qualities, didn't really do.

Once again Murray (first 20 seconds) and Smith (the rest) follow each other in an orderly fashion when it comes to the guitar solo section, but Murray takes the honours here with a scintillating burst which Smith, great as he is, cannot top.

'Prodigal Son' (Harris, Murray)

This six-minute track (the longest on the album) constitutes the only real stylistic break from the metal norm on the record. It's based around a bed of acoustic guitars, which is backed up by Harris's superbly fluid and lyrical bass lines. It isn't a 'power ballad' in the vein of 'Remember Tomorrow', nor even a quasi-psychedelic piece like 'Strange World', yet it is certainly closer to a balladic form than a metal song. There is a slight folk-rock influence with the way the acoustic guitars anchor proceedings, and Harris is certainly giving a little free rein to his love of progressive rock. There is enough time during the mid-song instrumental section for both guitarists to stretch out a little and take the opportunity of soloing over a slower chord progression, with Smith this time taking the lead for around forty seconds before Murray takes over. It is interesting to note just how similar a style they very often have, which allows them to follow each other almost seamlessly.

Lyrically things are a little confusing here, as the song, on the face of it, follows the biblical parable of the Prodigal Son, returning and repenting the sins of his earlier life. However, for some inexplicable reason, he is begging this forgiveness from a Lamia, which is a mythical female demon, normally represented as half-serpent, who preys on and devours children in the accepted mythology – surely something of an unlikely confessor to choose, one would think! It is likely that Harris was here influenced by the Genesis song 'The Lamia' from their 1974 album *The Lamb Lies Down on Broadway*, as he is known to have been an unashamed fan of the band.

Perhaps not a remarkable song in its own right, in the context of the album and its positioning in the running order, it is perfectly placed to give a little contrast and add some much-needed light and shade to proceedings. It's a nice track, and one which shows a softer side to Di'Anno's voice. It is one of only two songs on the album not composed solely by Harris. From the next album onward, writing credits would become much more varied.

'Purgatory' (Harris)
The first single released after the non-album 'Twilight Zone', this seems a rather odd choice to be honest. Very much a proto-speed metal track, with a riff similar in style to a couple of Deep Purple Mk.II's faster songs, there really isn't very much of a hook for a single-buying audience to latch onto at all. It's a decent enough speed rocker, all thing considered, but there's nothing very memorable about it. The record-buying public agreed, and it stalled at a lowly Number 52 in the UK singles chart. Of course, it didn't help that both this and the B-side – 'Genghis Khan' – were already on the album. Di'Anno seems to have trouble fitting the words into the space available again, at times, and as a result, his delivery comes across as rushed, and the lyric is very much obscured. This is a shame as, while clumsy in places, the words are interesting and certainly open to interpretation as to whether this is a dream or some sort of ghost story, or something else entirely. Annoyingly, after an interesting first verse and chorus, Harris does his Groundhog Day trick again of simply repeating the entire thing verbatim for the second half of the song. Murray handles the guitar solo here.

This was actually a rehash of a very early Maiden song, dating back to as early as 1978, called 'Floating' – the lyrics were changed somewhat but not entirely, and a reference to 'floating' still appears in the finished song. There is, however, no reference to 'purgatory' whatsoever, so the change of name seems rather odd to say the least. Short live clips of the original 'Floating' do exist, and it is recognisable as the same song, though played at a much slower tempo and with something of a reggae feel to it, as bizarre as that sounds! A halfway-decent recording of 'Floating' would prove fascinating indeed.

'Drifter' (Harris)

A much more upbeat and cheery way to close the album, with this track which had already seen live service on the reverse of the 'Sanctuary' single. Di'Anno is this time cast in the role of the hoary old clichéd drifter, who is born to keep on roaming, etc., etc. – the type of thing that David Coverdale practically trademarked at one time. Things are a little different here as, unlike the usual farewell to the woman he has to leave, on this occasion, our roaming friend is asking her to come with him. Her answer is not recorded in the lyric, but he does seem very excited about the prospect. It's fast and snappy, with a quite neat descending riff leading into the verses, but the best part of the whole track comes at the end of the first verse when things suddenly slow down out of nowhere to a sort of 'Bad Company ballad' feel, with Murray peeling off an absolutely beautiful bluesy solo as Di'Anno comes over all 'Paul Rodgers' in the background. It's out of left-field and absolutely stunning, though it doesn't last too long and never reappears again, with Smith's solo later in the song a much more typical fret-burning exercise, which is nevertheless extremely good.

The track was clearly written with the dreaded 'audience participation' in mind, as the line 'I'm gonna sing my song yeah, I want you to sing along' clearly leading to only one thing. This feature can be heard in the live version from 'Sanctuary'. It doesn't add anything, and the studio rendition is much better. On a side note, this is most certainly the only instance of an Iron Maiden song including the word 'cuddle' in its lyric, which I think the majority of people will agree, is the way it should stay.

Related songs:
'Twilight Zone' (Harris, Murray)

As with 'Sanctuary' on the debut, this track was a non-album single in the UK but was included on the US release a few months later. It only reached Number 31 in the singles chart, but it surely deserved better, as it is not only an excellent song but also quite catchy. Murray came up with the main riff for the song, while Harris wrote the melody and the words, which are very good. The unusual story concerns the spirit of a man who has been dead for a while but still returns to visit his lover and hopelessly wants to be with her, but he has no shape or form, and she cannot perceive that he is there. In a twist in the second verse, he admits that he is tempted to bring her over to the 'other side' with him – which would presumably entail killing her – but he cannot do it. It's half creepy, half tragic and fully entertaining! It also uses the word 'purgatory' as well as 'the twilight zone' to describe where he resides, which raises the possibility that the obtuse lyric to 'Purgatory' could be some kind of sequel or companion to this one

The mood of the music certainly belies the spirit (terrible pun intentional) of the song, as it clips along at quite a jolly pace, Di'Anno hitting the high notes like a young Ian Gillan, while some background harmony vocals recall Uriah Heep's distinctive use of the form. Interestingly, it has been claimed that Birch was unavailable at the time and the band had to produce this one themselves – if true, it's an excellent job. Great song, and very unfairly overlooked.

The other side of the single was 'Wrathchild', and in fact, in the UK it was a double A-side, for a rather unusual if practical reason. The band had no video or anything to accompany 'Twilight Zone', but they did have some live footage of themselves performing 'Wrathchild' at the Rainbow Theatre in London (which would appear on the 30-minute video *Live at the Rainbow* later that year). In case the song made the charts while they were away on tour, they figured that if 'Wrathchild' was also an A-side then at least *Top of the Pops* would have something to play. Sorry guys, it didn't become relevant this time!

Trivia fact: when the album was released in Japan, the Japanese record company people elected to include this song on it. Accordingly, Smallwood sent a telex over with lyrics and information about the song, and what it was about, helpfully headed 'Details of Twilight Zone'. Whoever received this message, or at least processed it, took this depressingly literally, and when the album appeared the track was listed under the title of 'Details of Twilight Zone'!

The Number of the Beast
Personnel:
Bruce Dickinson: vocals
Dave Murray: guitars
Adrian Smith: guitars
Steve Harris: bass guitar
Clive Burr: drums
Record Label: EMI (UK), Harvest (US)
Recorded: Jan-Feb 1982, produced by Martin Birch
Release date: 22 March 1982
Highest chart places: UK: 1, USA: 33
Running time: 39:11

The point at which everything changed. By the latter part of the lengthy tour promoting *Killers*, Paul Di'Anno had become something of a liability. Believing himself, like many of his peers, to be indestructible and capable of surviving the 'rock star' life, he had thrown himself headlong into a hedonistic daily whirl of booze and substance abuse, and his performances had become erratic at best. It could not continue and, following his last performance with the band, in Copenhagen on 10 September 1981, he was dismissed. The final straw, for Harris at least, had come when gigs had started having to be cancelled. Some things would not be tolerated, and that was right at the top of the list.

Bruce Dickinson had encountered Iron Maiden in 1980 when they were supporting his band Samson, and he was immediately massively impressed. As he said later, reported in Mick Wall's biography of Maiden, 'at that moment, I remember thinking... "I *know* I'm going to sing for that band!" ... I just thought "This is really me. Not Samson"'. Nevertheless, he continued to front Samson for another year and two albums, until a meeting with Maiden manager Rod Smallwood after Samson's set at the Reading Festival led to him being invited to audition. With Samson going through extensive management, financial and label problems at the time, it is little wonder that he accepted and, after performing 'Prowler', 'Sanctuary', 'Running Free' and 'Remember Tomorrow' at a rehearsal in Hackney in September 1981, he was hired.

Martin Birch for one was delighted, observing that it immediately became obvious that Harris had more freedom to write the songs he wanted to write without the restrictions of Di'Anno. Indeed, there was an immediate evolution of compositional style within the band as Dickinson's expansive range and versatility opened new doors. Dickinson could take no legal credit on the album in the way of writing, however, as a result of Samson's complicated contractual position at the time of his departure. He has since said that he did contribute to 'Children of the Damned', 'The Prisoner' and 'Run to the Hills'. The band continued the ongoing *Killers* tour until the end of the year, performing five of the new album's tracks as the dates went on and they began writing. The title track and 'Gangland' appear to be the only remaining songs

25

written after the tour finished in December.

Recording commenced in Battery Studios in January 1982, amid press reports about 'unexplained' events occurring, coinciding with the 'Satanic' theme of the album. These included lights turning off and on and gear breaking down before, ultimately, reports of Martin Birch having a car accident involving a mini-bus full of nuns and receiving a repair bill of £666! This is, of course, the type of thing that the popular press love to get their teeth into, and it is up to the reader how big they wish their pinch of salt to be regarding these 'phenomena'. The publicity certainly did the band's profile no harm, but it did result in somewhat more sinister attention as, when they visited the US, they ran into a storm of record-burning and 'bible belt' protesters causing havoc at many of the shows. One gig saw a 25-foot cross being carried in protest. These may well have largely been people who hadn't yet got over the popularity war between the Beatles and Jesus, but they certainly hadn't been paying attention to the lyrics on the album – which is not surprising given that their copies were on fire, I suppose. This reputation soon blew over, but it was a severe shock to the band at the time.

Album Cover:

As already discussed, the cover of the album was the artwork first submitted by Derek Riggs for the 'Purgatory' single, and the decision to hold it over for the album proved an excellent one as it is a truly iconic cover which would have been sadly wasted if consigned to the half-remembered archives of history on an unsuccessful single. Eddie is seen in easily his greatest guise yet, as the puppet-master controlling the strings of the devil. If you look closely, the devil himself can be seen controlling another smaller puppet, in the form of a tiny Eddie. The concept of this was explained by Riggs as a sort of 'Who's controlling who?' question, while he also claimed it was inspired by an old *Doctor Strange* comic book, which depicted Strange being controlled as a giant puppet in a similar way. The original vinyl cover was printed too light, with a blue rather than black finish to the chaotic sky behind the figures, with this being corrected years later when the album appeared on CD.

The rear cover showed the band standing on a flame-ravaged landscape like the one shown on the front, with Dickinson holding a burning torch as they look down into a fiery valley. A swirling void is in the sky behind them, while the track titles and a quote from the *Book of Revelations* are also shown. For the first time there was also a printed inner sleeve, with the lyrics on one side and strips of band photos on the other.

The two singles from the album also had similarly themed artwork. 'Run to the Hills' sported a battling Eddie and Satan atop a rocky promontory in Hell, which had nothing whatsoever to do with the lyrical content (though the fact that Eddie is using a tomahawk at least pays some lip-service), in a striking if somewhat ill-judged design. The title track appeared next with a sequel to that first image, with the clearly victorious Eddie holding aloft the severed head of his defeated demonic rival. I guess it is more appropriate this time, but it isn't actually all that good, with the expression on Satan's head particularly absurd. This design theme was wisely retired after this particular album's time period.

'Invaders' (Harris)

The origin of this one is no mystery, of course, as it is more or less an updated rewrite of the earlier 'Invasion'. It's certainly an improvement on its earlier incarnation and makes a decent fast in-your-face opener to the album, but Harris has since said that he would have preferred to replace it with something else if they had anything suitable available at that time. It certainly introduces Dickinson right away as being in a different class to Di'Anno as a pure vocalist, as his power and range are immediately apparent, not least his signature extended cry in 'stand your ground' during the first verse. Harris once again puts too many words in each line of the verses for it properly to scan, but to Dickinson's credit, he manages to squeeze in some very fast syllables with aplomb and clarity. The weakest part of the song is still, as it was previously, the chorus, with the 'Invaders ... pillaging / Invaders ... looting' template of lines badly interrupting the flow of the song. Murray followed by Smith take care of the guitar solo in that order.

The one place you would expect this song to really come into its own, even that chorus, would be on stage, with the audience singing along, but oddly enough the band have never played this version of the song live.

'Children of the Damned' (Harris)

A very different 'beast' (you knew I'd say that, didn't you?) to the opening track, this multi-faceted song is based on the 1963 film of the same name. A sequel of sorts to *Village of the Damned*, from three years previously, it concerns six children born with psychic powers who end up being destroyed by a combination of terror and fear. The song is set at the end of the film, when the children are killed, though it is not a literal depiction of the events in the film.

Musically, the song is a big step forward, with the opening verses accompanied by gentle acoustic guitars with a huge, slow, heavy chorus entering, repeating the title phrase with enormous power. Dickinson comes into his own here, and when the tempo picks up after this point to a faster, harder second section, he remains in absolute control. Smith takes the solo alone here before one final verse wraps things up, and we have had almost a mini-epic in just over four minutes. We're a long way from 'Running Free' or 'Sanctuary' here, and Harris is really warming to his task as an inventive and original wordsmith – at least as long as he keeps his lines short enough and doesn't repeat his verses, anyway!

'The Prisoner' (Smith, Harris)

More screen inspiration here, as Harris turns his inspirational sights on the television, with this song based on the cult 1960s series starring Patrick

McGoohan as the prisoner of the title, in the oddly surreal 'Village'. He is known only as 'Number Six', and matters are presided over by 'Number Two'. The track opens with a sample of dialogue from the original TV show, but rather than paint a picture of the actual Village and the plot, the lyric takes the show as its inspiration, using the image of the prisoner in the song to put across a message of freedom and defiance. It ends on a triumphant note, as the prisoner is now a free man, but in 1984 he would find himself 'Back in the Village' on the song of that name from the *Powerslave* album. The song itself is not quite classic Maiden, despite a very nice and powerful central riff, but the guitar solos (by Smith and then Murray) are magnificent, raising the whole track up a notch. It may be a little too long for its own good at six minutes, but it's certainly good stuff.

Permission had to be obtained from Patrick McGoohan himself to use the sample of dialogue at the beginning, and Rod Smallwood had the task of calling him on the phone one night to ask him, a task which he admits filled him with nerves. McGoohan agreed very readily, as it happened – apparently, he asked the name of the band, was told 'Iron Maiden' and responded simply with 'A rock band you say? ... (pause)... Do it!', before hanging up the phone.

'22 Acacia Avenue' (Harris, Smith)

... in which we take up the story of Charlotte (the Harlot) again, some years on, a new location but still doing what she does...

Musically, this is a great track for sure. Multi-faceted, with several sections of varying tempos which all somehow fit together, there is an atmospheric mid-section with a lovely Murray solo, while Smith gets to do the fret-burning on a ripping climactic excursion. The opening, chugging riff appears to bear a strong resemblance to 'Telegram' by Nazareth, from their 1976 album *Close Enough for Rock 'n' Roll*, and whether by accident or design it works very well. Lyrically this is altogether deeper and more mature than 'Charlotte the Harlot', to go with the much more complex music. The protagonist of the song goes beyond describing Charlotte's lascivious life and outlines what she is doing and why she should stop, painting a picture of how things might turn out when she is a little older. At the end of the song he volunteers to save her from her self-chosen life of vice and tells her 'you're packing your bags and you're coming with me'. But did she?

Interestingly, the song originally came from Adrian Smith's band Urchin, for whom he wrote it, albeit in a significantly different form. As he tells it, Steve Harris had seen Urchin play at an outdoor gig at their local park, and he remembered the song, and when Smith joined Maiden he asked about it, even humming it as the tune had stuck with him. Smith recognised it as '22 Acacia Avenue', and they turned it into its final form. There is a real lesson to be learned, as Smith himself said years later, in an interview with Mick Wall for his Maiden biography: 'We probably didn't even play well that day, and were probably really down afterwards, but because we had a go and did our best, someone in the audience remembered. That's why it always pays off to do your best, even if it seems like a dismal disaster at the time...'. Wise words indeed!

'The Number of the Beast' (Harris)
Ah yes, the track which half of the world seemed to decide to completely misinterpret at the time (though perhaps not entirely without some contribution from the band's own PR, with the tales of ghostly goings-on in the studio!). Essentially, the song, written by Harris alone, was inspired by a nightmare he had after watching the film *Damien: Omen II*. Now, it is strange that he should have had a nightmare induced by this particular film, as it is a fairly hopeless sequel – unless the nightmare was about the fact that he had wasted two hours watching it – but we'll let that pass. Harris has also claimed that there was some inspiration from the Robert Burns poem *Tam O'Shanter*.

The track opens with a voice intoning the biblical quotation from the rear cover, which as it happens is not only inaccurately quoted, but also comes from Chapters 12 and 13 in the *Book of Revelations*, and not all from Chapter 13 as credited. Nevertheless, it's an effective opener, even if it was recited by a lesser-known thespian and not Vincent Price, as was originally envisioned before – according to Dickinson – Vincent Priced himself out of the market. Nicely done in a very Vincent sort of way, though. The band enter with just the guitars first off, chugging along nicely as Dickinson, in his best vocal performance thus far, begins to relate what is, in fact, a cautionary tale of a Black Magic ceremony which he has happened to witness to his horror. As the full band come in, they are ushered in by a scream to rival even Roger Daltrey's legendary 'Won't Get Fooled Again' eruption. Blood-curdling stuff indeed, and the way the band kick into double tempo is masterful, and one of the great metal moments.

Two guitar solos come in at around the 2:45 mark, with the first, courtesy of Murray, particularly masterful. If one were to split hairs, the lyrics are occasionally a little clunky. 'This can't go on, I must inform the law' is a little on the feeble side when The Great Beast is being invoked, as the arrival of a policeman on the beat would be unlikely to help, but overall the words do their job in carrying the menace of the music. If there is one particular line which could be said to have encouraged the record-burning brigade more than any other, it is the final chorus of '666 – the number of the beast / 666 – the one for you and me', which, when taken out of context, does sound as if it is being encouraged somewhat. Still, people who arrive at gigs carrying a 25-foot cross don't generally need a whole lot of encouragement, I imagine.

There was an official video for the single, which mainly intersperses footage of the band playing on stage with clips of old horror movies – as well as a bizarre moment when a ballroom-dancing couple twirl across the stage past the band in nimble-footed mode, before the female dancer turns into a werewolf, but only from the neck up. That's an effects budget for you. They hold up cards marking themselves as – come on, you guessed it – 6-6-6. It's cheap and cheerful but puts the song over well, and you can just tell from Harris's expression that he simply knew that this was how they turned the corner. Overall, a metal classic, few would argue.

Side note: six years after the recording, the spine-chilling narrator on the track, English actor Barry Clayton, went on to his most long-running and best-remembered job. As the narrator of *Count Duckula*. There's a message in there somewhere, but I'm not sure what it is.

'Run to the Hills' (Harris)

Speaking of metal classics, here's another one right on the heels of the Beast. To this day perhaps the Maiden song most recognised by the general public, it made Number Seven on the UK singles chart on its release as the first single from the album. It's easily understandable, as the chorus is one of those great Dickinson / Maiden examples of a soaring chorus that simply takes flight irresistibly. The song is introduced by Clive Burr's drums before an immediately catch if simple guitar figure carries the first verse. At this point, things get really interesting as the first real classic example of that famous Maiden 'gallop' comes in, with the next verse accompanied by a breathless rhythm very reminiscent of horses charging into battle. So far so good, but then... that chorus. Oh my word! It is almost impossible not to find oneself bellowing along, certainly by the end of the song, by which time it has been taken to new heights of anthemic splendour. With Murray taking the solo in equally stirring style, and Burr excelling in the chorus, it's marvellous stuff.

Lyrically it is equally impressive, with the song looking at the subjugation of the indigenous Native American people by the white settlers, uniquely seen from both sides in different verses. There was a widely-shown official video which saw the band puncturing the serious nature of the lyric by mixing live footage with extremely funny old black-and-white comedy Western footage. The message of the song is powerful and still relevant today, but nevertheless, it is hard to resist clips of 'Indian' braves riding on a four-seater bicycle firing arrows or, best of all, the moment when one of them creeps up behind someone and grabs his hair to scalp him, only for the man's toupee to come off in his hand! A great early example of Maiden not taking themselves too seriously, and a great single. The mainstream success, and the foothold in America, began here.

Though credited solely to Harris, Dickinson has been reported as having made a significant contribution to the song, though contractually unable to receive credit. In 1982 he was quoted as saying that the song in part is based on the 'rising sixth' interval within a scale, inspired by a documentary he watched which explored why 'My Way' was so popular. The forum he used to deliver this scholarly observation was when he was speaking at the IBM Smarter Business conference in Stockholm, in 2002. Now, that may not be particularly 'rock and roll', but it's certainly impressive...

'Gangland' (Smith, Burr)

The only real misstep on the album, apart arguably from, 'Invaders', this tale of gang warfare, possibly based on the Kray Twins and the like in the band's own East End, is musically very simplistic and comes across as something which would have fitted into Di'Anno's more direct style. It clatters along enjoyably enough in its way, but it is forgettable. Indeed, the band themselves have remarked that, when finalising the album, they had to choose between this track and 'Total Eclipse' for which should go on the album and which should be relegated to the B-side of 'Run to the Hills'. They have also stated that they believe they got it wrong. The solo is taken by Smith, but in truth, the most notable thing about the track is that it is the only song on a Maiden album to be co-written by Clive Burr (his slightly jazzy touches are noticeable on here). The only other song he received a credit on was the aforementioned non-album 'Total Eclipse'.

'Hallowed Be Thy Name' (Harris)

Almost certainly the most revered track by Maiden fans from the album, this closing seven-minute epic is still played at almost every Maiden show to this day and has demonstrated a lasting quality that some of the earlier material simply could not offer. Written from the point of view of a man who is about to be executed, the lyrics take us through his every emotion, from lamenting his position, through to fear, denial, rage at God and finally an acceptance that he is not afraid of dying since he is certain that death is not the end. It is a very powerful piece of writing, and probably Harris's best lyric up to this time.

Musically, it takes us through the whole range of stylistic moods. These begin with the laid back, yet dramatic, opening with the tolling bell interrupting mournful guitar, through the point when the band come in taking the same theme to faster and heavier levels and going through a commanding vocal performance from Dickinson. After the final verse, the song breaks down to restrained drama again before bursting into a driving, unstoppable double-tempo conclusion, including superb solos from first Murray and then, possibly even better, Smith. Toward the end, Dickinson comes in again, howling the song title repeatedly, as if to commend himself into the hands of God as the executioner takes him. It's stunning stuff, and in the live environment it takes on even more power and emotional pummelling. No wonder they still like to play it at the end of the live shows – it's almost like their own 'Stairway to Heaven', such is its connection with the audience.

It's worth noting that, while the lyrics are superbly written, the old Harris habit of putting too many words into some lines does persist, and Dickinson can be heard dropping the odd word here and there, just to make it scan. He has to allow the line 'Mark my words please believe my soul lives on' to bleed over into the next, such is the impossibility of cramming in the syllables. It's certainly not like 'Phantom of the Opera', but the tendency is still there. Mind you, it's a habit shared (in even worse form) by Bernie Taupin over the years, and he's done all right for himself!

Ending the album on this note was an almost tangible invitation to other bands to 'Come on then, beat that!', and to the metal audience, 'Okay, resist that then!' In both cases the answer was largely a resounding, 'Nope, we won't even try!' Maiden had arrived on the world stage.

Related songs:
'Total Eclipse' (Harris, Murray, Burr)
The B-side to the 'Run to the Hills' single, this is the song which lost out to 'Gangland' in the 'last album spot' shootout. And as the band have agreed themselves, it shouldn't have. It isn't the greatest song from the *Beast* sessions, but it's far from the worst. It has another ambitious lyric, telling of a world facing an ecological apocalypse, a message still relevant today. Lines such as 'War babies in the Garden of Eden shall turn our ashes to ice' show a real growth in the quality and maturity of the Maiden (and Harris) lyrics. Musically, there is little of the grandstanding express tempo thing, except for one slightly clumsy transition into the guitar solos (Murray, then Smith). Instead, the song switches between slow, stately heavy riffing (a little reminiscent of Black Sabbath's 'Snowblind'), and a mid-tempo groove driving the verses along with an irresistible momentum. The song was added to the album belatedly upon the remaster in 1998, just before 'Hallowed Be Thy Name', but it should have been done from the word 'go'.

'Remember Tomorrow (Live)' (Harris, Di'Anno)
An unexpected rendition of this song from the debut album graced the flip side of the 'Number of the Beast' single. It has been the subject of conjecture since, however, as the origin of the recording has been called into question. The band, and Rod Smallwood, have all claimed that the track was recorded in 1981, shortly after Bruce joined the band. However, it has been asserted strongly that the recording is, in fact, the exact same one which appeared on the *Maiden Japan* EP, with Paul Di'Anno singing it, and that his vocals were replaced by a new vocal recorded in the studio by Dickinson. This theory has a lot of credence as a close listen to the two tracks reveals them to sound exactly the same apart from the vocal, and they are also the same length. Also the same 'Thank you very much' can be heard at the end, so it would seem that it had been left on in the editing process. It seems a rather strange thing to do if this is indeed the case, but back to back listening to the two recordings certainly supports it.

Piece Of Mind

Personnel:
Bruce Dickinson: vocals
Dave Murray: guitars
Adrian Smith: guitars
Steve Harris: bass guitar
Nicko McBrain: drums
Record Label: EMI (UK), Capitol (US)
Recorded: Feb-March 1983, produced by Martin Birch
Release date: 16 May 1983
Highest chart places: UK: 3, USA: 14
Running time: 45:18

Following the Beast on the Road tour, in December 1982, another line-up
change hit the band when Clive Burr was dismissed and replaced by Nicko
McBrain, who had recently left the band Trust. However, the truth of this
change is to this day shrouded in whispers and contradiction. The band
claimed that Burr was beginning to let his performances suffer after he started
to indulge too much in the rock and roll lifestyle, in a similar way to Paul
Di'Anno (only more alcohol and less cocaine). That was the story which was
seized upon by the press, but Clive himself, right up to his death in 2013,
insisted that this was not the case. As he always told it, during the American
leg of the tour, in the Autumn of 1982, with the band supporting Judas Priest,
Burr received a call asking him to return to London as his father had passed
away. He claimed the rest of the band were more than supportive, insisting he
go, and they got McBrain in as a temporary stand-in for two weeks – something
Clive was happy about, as he knew and liked Nicko. When he returned,
however, he claimed things had changed, and the atmosphere wasn't the
same, and that as soon as the tour ended, he was dismissed as they felt it was
'time for a change'. He always denied excessive alcohol use and believed that
the band simply found they liked playing with Nicko, using the tales of his
indiscipline as an excuse.

We will probably never know the real truth, as Clive has now sadly passed
away from complications associated with Multiple Sclerosis, with which he
had been diagnosed in the early '90s. Happily, he was completely reconciled
with the band after this shocking diagnosis, as they played benefit gigs (under
the 'Clive Aid' banner) and raised vital money, not only for his treatment and
living adaptations but also for many other MS sufferers. Coincidentally, when
he left Maiden, Clive played with Trust, replacing Nicko there just as Nicko was
replacing him in Maiden. He went on to record and play with other bands,
such as Elixir and Praying Mantis, but never again reached the heights of his
Maiden days.

Nicko McBrain had been a friend and fan of Maiden for some time,
occasionally appearing onstage as 'Eddie', so in many ways, he was a natural

fit. Having made his album recording debut back in 1973 on the album *Giltrap* by Gordon Giltrap, he went on to play with bands such as Streetwalkers and The Pat Travers Band before Trust and Maiden came along. Interestingly, in 1973 he had also played on a single associated with Tottenham Hotspur Football Club, called 'Nice One Cyril' after the player Cyril Knowles, with a band credited as The Cockerel Chorus. This contrasts sharply with Steve Harris's outspoken and fanatical support of London rivals West Ham United, who are also known as 'The Irons', inspiring Harris to come up with the band slogan 'Up the Irons'. McBrain was initially named Michael but was given the nickname 'Nicky' after a teddy bear he owned as a child, called Nicholas, which later evolved into Nicko.

When McBrain joined the band in December 1982, they quickly decamped to Jersey, where they took over an off-season hotel called Le Chalet, rehearsing in the hotel restaurant. Writing complete, they headed to the Bahamas in February to record the album at Compass Point Studios in Nassau – somewhat more exotic than their previous location of Battery Studios in North London! The album, again produced by Martin Birch, received extremely positive reviews when released in May 1983, reaching the band's best US chart position yet (14), while also hitting Number 3 in the UK. The World Piece tour to promote the record began in Hull on 2 May and featured 139 shows between then and December. Quite the schedule!

Album Cover:

Riggs once again here, of course, and also once again Eddie taking centre stage, this time in a lobotomised form, chained and clad in a straitjacket in a padded room. This began the tradition of Eddie having a metal plate and bolts on his forehead from this point on. The image wraps around onto the back of the gatefold to reveal a door in the cell, opening onto what looks somewhat like the sky from the *Number of the Beast* cover. The track details are also on the reverse, along with the band line-up and another quote from the *Book of Revelations*, deliberately amended to replace the words 'any more pain' with 'any more brain' in reference to the title. In fact, on this occasion, the concept for the cover had been generated by Harris with manager Rod Smallwood, and from their outline, Riggs actually came out to Nassau to paint it for them while they were recording. Any excuse, one might remark! The original working title had been 'Food for Thought' before *Piece of Mind* was inspired both by the cover idea and a band meeting in a pub in Jersey! The Riggs logo can be seen here on a locket held in a disembodied hand, though it is missing on the CD release. The inner gatefold featured the band seated around an opulent dining table on the left panel, with the lyrics on the right.

Riggs also designed the covers for the two singles from the album. 'Flight of Icarus', featuring a flamethrower-wielding flying Eddie burning Icarus' wings, and 'The Trooper', with its iconic and stunning image of Eddie as 19th Century British soldier wielding a tattered flag. Note that the figure of Icarus resembles the Icarus painting by William Rimmer which was used by Led Zeppelin for their Swan Song record label. According to Riggs, this was a deliberate tip of the hat to Zeppelin, who had split up two-and-a-half years earlier.

'Where Eagles Dare' (Harris)

Once again Harris turns his attention to literary matters in this stunning album opener. Based on the Alistair MacLean novel from 1967 (and film from the following year starring Richard Burton), this time out he takes a literal, storytelling approach, outlining the daring assault on a Nazi stronghold high in the Bavarian Alps. It's six minutes long, but there is barely a moment wasted.

One can imagine how many listeners must have put this on the turntable, only to immediately nod and think 'Ah, so THAT'S why they brought in Nicko!' because his drum work on the track is so good that it single-handedly raises it from the status of 'good album opener' to greatness. The very beginning of the song is a deceptively complex drum intro which he apparently nailed in seconds after a full day spent perfecting a completely different one. Harris came in the following morning, heard it and said 'no, something more like this', to which the final piece was immediately delivered.

Dickinson excels again, relating the story with just the right amount of excitement and suspense, despite some very wordy lines again. There is a long instrumental section, containing solos by Murray and then Smith which are superb in themselves, but the real star is the constant underpinning of the fairly simple chord progression by Nicko's insistent machine-gun pattern. If ever a song was likely to induce an attack of involuntary 'air-drumming', this is the one. There are one or two slightly clumsy lines, and the old scanning problem hits Bruce again when the word 'valley' has room for only one syllable while 'Eagle's Nest' in the next line calls for one too many, but he navigates it well, and such is the breathless urgency and sheer quality of the track – together with the commendable literary intent of the subject matter – that criticism would be pointless. This is Maiden getting better and better.

'Revelations' (Dickinson)

The first Maiden song credited to Bruce alone – and what a start! Much has been said of the intelligence and literacy of Harris's words, but this one takes it one step further into an obliquely written reflection on such matters as free will, comparative religion, good versus evil and such theological matters. The song opens with a verse from a hymn by G. K. Chesterton, chosen by Bruce as he felt it had continued relevance to the modern world, with its plea to God to take away our chains formed of pride and money, among other things. The next verse opens with a direct reference to the black magician Aleister Crowley, with the line 'Just a babe in a black abyss', as the phrase 'babe in the black abyss' was used by Crowley himself, in his book *Liber Cheth vel Vallum Abiegni*, to reference a rank of spirituality. There are other Crowley references sprinkled in the text which, given the message that seems to be laid out in parts of the song regarding the hidden danger of following religious leaders blindly, would fit with Crowley's creed of 'Do what thou wilt shall be the whole of the law'. Fascinating hints abound within the cryptic words, such as 'The Eyes of the Nile are opening, you'll see', which could well be a warning of the danger mentioned above; the Eyes of the Nile are what the Egyptians used to call the eyes of the hunting crocodiles at night, which were the only parts visible and shone in the moonlight, and this would be a powerful metaphor for hidden danger. Elsewhere there is a line about 'the venom which tears my spine', and Dickinson has confirmed that this relates to the Hindu belief that a serpent ('Kundalini') lies dormant at the base of everybody's spine, and when this worm is awakened by the 'Samadhi' (a spiritual entity created by orgasm or intense meditation) the serpent makes its way up the spinal cord and releases its venom into the brain, creating a union with God, and therefore this may be the meaning of the Eyes of the Nile opening, relating to new possibilities opening up.

Of course, how exactly these diverse references fit together is something known only to Dickinson himself. What is 'the secret of the Hanged Man' (or is it 'hangman'?), and the smile upon his lips? This could be a reference to 'Hallowed Be Thy Name', and the protagonist's welcoming of the noose as it will join him to God, but Bruce Dickinson has said that it refers to the tarot card The Hanged Man and that the smile relates to the fact that in the Hindu tradition the card is supposed to represent good luck. There are nods to the Sun and Moon, representing masculinity and femininity, and at the very end 'The one who would be King, the watcher in the ring' is followed by the climactic 'It is you, it is you', appearing to indicate that ultimately we should follow our own souls where they lead us. Note that there are also two further lines from the Chesterton hymn used within the song, namely 'bind all of our lives together' and 'ablaze with hope and free', which become the line 'bind all of us together, ablaze with hope and free'. Thoughtful, intelligent, literate and obliquely subtle, this is devastatingly good songwriting, and that only covers the lyrics!

Musically, this is equally impressive, covering all bases over its near seven-minute running time. There are slow heavy sections (the opening Chesterton verse), quiet meditative verses, dramatic great heavy choruses and plenty of intricate and proggy harmonic twin guitar work to lift it above the norm. Of course, few Maiden songs would be really complete without that great shift up in tempo, and that is used on a couple of occasions here. Firstly it is used at around the two-minute mark, before the first verse proper, and later to usher in the instrumental section, heralded by Bruce's 'Go!', before superb guitar solos by Murray and then Smith lift things still further. Murray, in particular, had taken his playing to a whole new level since the relatively raw work on the early albums. Two songs in, and two masterpieces. This is a very special start to an album indeed.

'Flight of Icarus' (Smith, Dickinson)
Another Dickinson lyric here, this time reinterpreting the Greek mythological take of Icarus, who had a pair of wings, made with his father Daedalus but

flew too close to the Sun so that the wax in the wings melted. It isn't a straight retelling, as there are glaring differences: in the song, Icarus takes to the air encouraged by his father, as a crowd looks on, whereas in the original story there was no crowd, and they, in fact, both flew as a means to escape the labyrinth of the minotaur. Dickinson has said that he twisted the tale slightly to turn it into an allegory about teenage rebellion, which in the case of Icarus led to his death. There is one line 'now he knows his father betrayed', just before his wings 'turn to ashes', which leaves the question open as to whether this means his father betrayed him (with faulty wings), whether his father was betrayed by someone who helped him, or indeed whether it is he who has 'betrayed' his father's belief in him by flying too close to the Sun as in the original tale. Of course, on the cover of the single, it is Eddie with a flamethrower, but we'll let that particular reinterpretation slide!

The song was released as the first single from the album and reached Number Eleven in the UK charts as well as gaining significant airplay in the US (it scored highly on the rock charts). It certainly opened doors, but it was a bone of contention between Dickinson and Harris. The song is taken at a relatively relaxed pace, with the chorus big, anthemic and standing proud from the song, but Harris wanted to take it at a faster pace, which is the way it was subsequently played live. Dickinson, however, stood firm, insisting that the way it was would get it onto the radio in America and be a help to their career. Ultimately, he was right.

The song is co-written by Adrian Smith but, despite this, Murray takes more of the limelight, playing the first of two relatively short mid-song solos and then a later solo to himself. He does it brilliantly, though. There was an official video for the song, filmed in the studio in Nassau and depicting the band running through a staged recording. Notable on this film is the sight of an astonishingly young-looking Nicko behind the drumkit, who also takes the part of a rather blue-tinged Grim reaper, while Martin Birch also has a cameo, changing into Eddie and back again in a flash. Dickinson's vocal on this one has a little of the feel of Ronnie James Dio in parts, which is never a bad thing. His delivery of the line 'In the name of God my father, I'll fly!' is so impassioned it makes Bono's 'Tonight thank God it's them instead of you' from the Band Aid single sound like Kraftwerk.

'Die With Your Boots On' (Smith, Dickinson, Harris)
A three-way co-write this time, with Dickinson again involved along with Smith and Harris, who is back in the frame after an unusual run of two songs without his input. In this case, the message of the song is concerning a vision of an apocalyptic future, taking its inspiration straight from the Cold War fears of nuclear escalation which were so prevalent at the time. Nostradamus is referred to in the second verse in terms of prophecy, and the song is effectively telling people that listening to leaders or prophets of disaster and asking them for answers is pointless and that the best course of action is to live life

regardless, and figuratively 'die with your boots on'.

Musically this is much more straightforward fare, being a straight-ahead, meat and potatoes Iron Maiden charger, pretty much from start to finish. And nothing wrong with that! The chorus is Maiden at their absolute fire-engine best, only marred by some dreadful backing vocals intoning 'if you're gonna die', and sounding as if a few mates of theirs had stumbled back with them from the pub and 'had a go'! This is odd, as the band's backing vocals are usually well done and unobtrusive, but in this case, they really interrupt the force of nature which is Bruce in full flight. According to Harris, his only contribution was the chord sequence in the verses, while the lyrics were the work of Dickinson, with the main riff being courtesy of Dickinson and Smith. It's a good song apart from that vocal issue, albeit not the band's most adventurous moment, and it did make a great on-stage number.

'The Trooper' (Harris)

If the previous track perhaps didn't end Side One of the vinyl album in truly classic style, there can be no mistake about this, the opening to the second side. Released as the second single from the album, and reaching Number Twelve in the UK singles charts, 'The Trooper' has become one of the most popular, most recognisable and most regularly played of all Maiden songs, and not without good reason.

The song, by Harris, was written to depict the Crimean battle known as The Charge of the Light Brigade and was inspired by the Tennyson poem of the same name. The famous charge occurred as an error in communication, when the commander, Lord Raglan, gave the order to retake some British guns which were being retrieved by the Russian forces. The cavalry on the ground could not see what he could from his elevated position and could not tell which guns were being referred to, as Raglan did not specify this, believing it to be obvious. Thus, under the command of Lord Cardigan, who refused to listen to a messenger informing him of his mistake, the 647 mounted cavalrymen obeyed his suicidal order to instead directly charge upon the Russian guns in the valley. In fact, the Russian forces were so astonished by this move that they did not begin firing immediately, but when they did, it was a massacre. Out of 647 mounted men, 195 survived – including, ironically, Lord Cardigan, whose blinkered arrogance led to the catastrophe. To compound this, when he realised what was happening, Cardigan was first to ride out of the fray and left his men behind him to find their own way back. This is the event behind the famous line from the poem 'Into the valley of death rode the six hundred', and the song perfectly encapsulates this mayhem and slaughter. It also draws attention to the futile bravery of men and the sometimes wilfulness of their officers.

The lyric to the song may well be poignant and historically instructive, but the main thrust musically is the evocation of the battle, and the charge itself, and it does so in exceptional fashion. Beginning with the track's main 'hook', the brilliant twin lead guitar riff, the first verse begins in stop/start manner, Dickinson singing the lines acapella as the band enter between each line in a staccato effect. However, after this they kick in with perhaps the ultimate example of the trademark Iron Maiden 'gallop', and the listener is swept along in unstoppable excitement, as if on one of those ill-fated horses themselves. If 'Run to the Hills' had been the first to evoke that galloping rhythm, this made it seem like a canter in comparison. There is simply no let-up in the track at all, with guitar solos by Smith first (one of his best to this point) and then Murray only serving to speed things along. In a live setting, the song is a veritable force of nature: Iron Maiden, writ large and in the raw.

There was an official video made for the single, with the band again shown playing the track (on a rather striking black and white chequerboard stage, no less), interspersed superbly with action scenes from the 1936 Errol Flynn film *The Charge of the Light Brigade.* This is similar to the way the old footage was woven into the 'Run to the Hills' video, but this time with no laughs whatsoever. Opening and closing with lines from the poem as full-screen captions, the footage is edited to, at times, mirror exactly what Bruce is singing, and as such is doubly effective. The BBC complained and insisted the video was too violent to be shown unedited, which for something using 1936 footage seems laughable. Thin Lizzy's song 'Massacre' was inspired by the same battle, and it is notable that Maiden later covered that song. In recent years the song title has given its name to the official Iron Maiden beer, 'Trooper', which also uses the iconic image of Eddie as British soldier for its label.

Interestingly, there is an old and slightly obscure version of the US Confederate flag which depicts a sort of skeleton figure going into battle for the South, carrying a Confederate flag himself and adopting an almost identical pose to that of Eddie in the famous illustration. It may be a coincidence, but the similarity is striking enough to question whether Riggs may have taken inspiration from this image.

'Still Life' (Murray, Harris)
A different approach with this track as Harris relates a tale of a man who becomes obsessed with the spirits he sees in a pool of water, eventually losing his mind and jumping in to join them, taking his partner with him where they both drown. There have been a lot of claims over the years that the song was inspired by the plot of a short story by horror writer Ramsay Campbell called 'The Inhabitant Of The Lake, written when he was only 18 in fact. Steve Harris has never (to my knowledge) confirmed or denied this, only going so far as to say that the idea sprang from his fear of drowning. The song also conjures up the image of the Dead Marshes in J. R. R. Tolkien's *The Lord of the Rings*, with the spirits therein calling for Frodo to come in and join them in death.

The song starts with a very atmospheric, mellow opening, with Dave Murray's eerie guitar work conjuring up images which certainly bring to mind the Dead Marshes as mentioned above. This part of the song could have been used in the film adaptation without any problem! The guitar slowly builds up alongside Dickinson's voice on the first few lines, before it rocks up, although not to the tempo or heaviness of something like 'The Trooper' or 'Die With Your Boots On'. The chorus is very strong, and it continues the second side in a very strong manner. The guitar solo section mid-song is in three parts, with a short twin-lead section followed by Smith and then Murray.

At the beginning of the track is some speech recorded backwards. Done as a tongue-in-cheek response to the fanatics denouncing their music as Satanic, the message actually consists of a rather inebriated McBrain replicating comedian John Bird's imitation of Ugandan leader Idi Amin. The words he actually utters are 'What ho said the t'ing with the three "bonce", don't meddle wid t'ings yo don't understand...', followed by a belch! Highly Satanic...

Note that although this was the first Maiden album not to be named after a song on the record, 'Still Life' does contain the title after a fashion, in the line 'Nightmares ... give me peace of mind'.

'Quest for Fire' (Harris)

If there is a whiff of filler at any point on the album, this is where it arrives, with this rather slight and inconsequential song based on the 1981 film of the same name (in turn based on a 1911 book by Belgian author J. H. Rosny – the pseudonym of Joseph Henri Honoré Boex). The film and book revolve around the quest of a group of primitive men to regain the source of the fire they believed lost and takes as its theme that of personal growth and development. The song has none of these subtleties in its two scant verses, and opening with the hilariously absurd line 'In a time when dinosaurs walked the earth' does nothing for its credibility right off the bat. Of course, dinosaurs had died out millions of years before man arrived, and indeed neither the book nor the film contain any, so it is difficult to understand this bizarre inclusion. The line 'to search for landscapes men would roam' also seems odd since there does not appear to be any sort of quest for any sort of new 'landscapes' involved.

Leaving all of that aside, what of the music, which of course is the primary feature of a song. It is also inconsequential, unfortunately, with a sort of chugging 'Maiden-by-numbers' verse giving way to a rather banal 'Drawn by quest for fire...' chorus. It was better on stage but did not remain in the set for very long.

'Sun and Steel' (Dickinson, Smith)

Another relatively slight song, this is a better track than 'Quest for Fire' when taken for what it is – namely a simple and relatively unchallenging Maiden piece with a catchy chorus. The lyric, by Dickinson, again has lofty ideals, being inspired by the great Samurai warrior Miyamoto Musashi, who is said to have killed his first man at the age of thirteen, as referenced in the lyric. Late in life, he wrote the famous combat guide *The Book of Five Rings*, which is divided into five sections, the books of Earth, Water, Fire, Wind and The Void – the first four of which are alluded to in the lyric. The song describes him as striving for death either in combat or (as claimed by Harris) by 'hara-kiri' (ritual suicide). That being the case, he would appear to have been somewhat unsuccessful, as he died aged 61 in 1645, from what is believed to have been lung cancer.

Musically the track is reminiscent of 'Quest for Fire', with the propulsive verses leading into the hook-laden chorus, which is good enough, if repeated far too often. By Dickinson's standards and those of the band themselves, it is fun, if unremarkable. It has never been played live.

'To Tame a Land' (Harris)

An epic to finish the album off, in the shape of this seven-and-a-half-minute Harris song. Lyrically, it is summarising the science fiction novel *Dune* by Frank Herbert, a favourite of Harris, though this, of course, would be somewhat lost on anyone unfamiliar with the book. Many people might be aware of the sandworms which feature in the Herbert book and are referenced in the song, but most of the rest is aimed squarely at the aficionado. To put it in a very small nutshell, the book centres around the planet Arrakis, the only source of a sought-after spice, and the political trials and machinations to control it. The Fremen are the native inhabitants, while the 'king' described in the song is Paul Atreides, the hero of the novel, who becomes the Kwizatz Haderach, a 'super-being' title, after gaining powers of clairvoyance across time and space.

Musically, the song begins with a slow and mysterious sounding guitar and bass intro adapted from the classical guitar piece 'Asturias' by the Spanish composer Isaak Albeniz – 'Spanish Caravan' by the Doors also notably adapts part of this piece – before the band enter and take us through the vocal section of the track, lasting around three minutes and pretty powerful with a quite catchy vocal melody in parts. In some ways, the real meat of the track begins at the four-minute mark, from where the second half is taken up by a lengthy, fast-tempo instrumental section incorporating over a minute of duelling guitar solos, from Murray and then Smith. The 'Asturias' theme is referenced again, subtly, during this much faster part, especially during Murray's solo. Gradually toward the end of the track things slow down again before the introductory section comes in again to gradually let us down for a gentle landing. It is a superb way to end the album, and a great example among many of how important Harris is, with his bass lines really driving the song and giving it much of its character. He has said that he tended to write on bass, which goes some way to explaining how identifiable his style is.

The reason for the title of the song, rather than it being called 'Dune', as you may expect, is an unfortunate one. Superfan Harris wanted to name the song after the novel and had even considered using a spoken word passage from the book as an introduction, so Frank Herbert was duly contacted, politely, to ask for permission. The reply from Herbert, via his agent, read as follows: 'No. Because Frank Herbert doesn't like rock bands, particularly heavy rock bands, and especially rock bands like Iron Maiden'. I think we can all say 'ouch' at this point! Now, it certainly would have been entirely understandable at that point if Harris had decided that the good Mr Herbert could stick his free global publicity where the sandworms don't burrow, and instead written a different set of lyrics. To his credit, however, and the delight of the many metal fans who loved the book, he kept it as it was and dutifully altered the title. The slight was not forgotten, however, with Dickinson sometimes turning his ire on Herbert when introducing the song in concert, and especially so on one extremely outspoken occasion in Sweden in June 1983, describing the writer with a derogatory word which I will elect not to quote!

Related songs:
'I've Got the Fire' (Montrose)
The B-side to 'Flight of Icarus', this is a studio recording of a Montrose song (from their 1974 album *Paper Money*, which had previously seen Maiden action as a live recording on the 12" version of the 'Sanctuary' single. This effort is succinct and to the point (under three minutes) and is certainly tighter and punchier than that previous version, but it's a rather simplistic song for Maiden to cover at this point in their career, and it doesn't really suit Bruce's voice. Commenting on the track in the booklet accompanying the album *Best of the 'B' Sides*, Rod Smallwood clearly gets confused about the two versions, describing this one as a live version with Di'Anno.

'Cross-Eyed Mary' (Anderson)
On the reverse of 'The Trooper', another cover version, this time from the even more unlikely source of Jethro Tull. Unlikely, that is, until you discover that both Harris and Dickinson were massive fans of the band. Drawn from the album *Aqualung*, and referencing that album's title character in the lyric, this sordid and cynical take of a schoolgirl prostitute is interpreted extremely well, with the use of guitar instead of flute in the intro lending an inspired twist. Overall it is just prevented from matching the original because Dickinson's voice, great as it is, cannot come near to the mocking and sardonic sneer of Ian Anderson's vocal. Very entertaining, though, and an interesting choice for a B-side, for sure.

Powerslave

Personnel:
Bruce Dickinson: vocals
Dave Murray: guitars
Adrian Smith: guitars
Steve Harris: bass guitar
Nicko McBrain: drums
Record Label: EMI (UK), Capitol (US)
Recorded: Feb-June 1984, produced by Martin Birch
Release date: 3 September 1984.
Highest chart places: UK: 2, USA: 21
Running time: 51:12

In which Iron Maiden release their first-ever album with the same personnel
as the previous one! This would be followed by a further two studio releases
before the next upheaval was to happen.

But that is, of course, for later.

In January 1984, after the completion of the World Piece tour in December,
the band took a rare three weeks off, before they regrouped once again at Le
Chalet hotel in Jersey, following the pattern of *Piece of Mind*, as they wrote
and rehearsed for the upcoming album there in the empty, off-season hotel.
Also following the model of the previous album, they headed over to Compass
Point Studios in Nassau again (and why not?) to begin recording. Following
completion of recording, the album was mixed at Electric Lady Studios in New
York, before the band began rehearsing for the accompanying World Slavery
Tour.

Beginning in August 1984 in Poland, of all unlikely places, this jaunt was to
be the band's most arduous yet, lasting for eleven months and taking in 28
countries and 178 shows. These included future strongholds for the band such
as Brazil and other South American locations, which began cottoning on to
the group with this breakthrough album. In the UK it went into the charts at
Number Two but was kept off the top spot by the third in their own label EMI's
pop compilation series *Now That's What I Call Music*. Now that's what I call
depressing! Along with the shows behind the Iron Curtain, beginning with that
first show in Warsaw, the other groundbreaking date on the tour was the first
Rock In Rio festival, where the band played to 350,000 people and, according
to Bruce Dickinson, essentially 'conquered an entire continent overnight with
that one show'. It was a long way from The Ruskin Arms in the East End, that's
for sure.

Album Cover:

In many people's eyes, this Egyptian masterpiece still represents the apex
of Derek Riggs' work for the band. The front cover sported a sumptuous
illustration of a massive pyramid, fronted by Eddie as an enormous Pharaoh

figure flanked by four others gracing this opulent shrine. From the scale of the pyramid and figures through to the stunning walkway to the front and the crackling electricity from the lightning striking the apex, the work is breathtaking. However, look closer, and the band's sense of humour can be seen pricking the pomposity via several images which are hidden among the hieroglyphs. 'Bollockz' and 'Wot a load of crap' are two hidden directly in the hieroglyphs, above figures which resemble dogs with long blond hair, and there is also a crudely drawn Mickey Mouse, graffiti reading 'Indiana Jones was here 1941' and a drawing of the wartime character Chad looking over a wall and asking 'Wot? No Guinness'. You would be unlikely to find that with Yes or Led Zeppelin, I would venture to suggest!

The rear cover features Pharaoh Eddie again, this time as a sarcophagus, lying in stark fashion in the foreground, with a host of Egyptian markings and icons in the background. The inner sleeve had a photo of the band standing next to a gold sarcophagus on one side, with the lyrics on the other emblazoned with the eye of Horus. No gatefold this time out, but there would later be a gatefold vinyl release, giving away its later origin by featuring live shots from the World Slavery tour on its inner spread.

There were two accompanying single releases, both also with Riggs covers. '2 Minutes to Midnight' depicted a military Eddie with machine gun sitting before a nuclear explosion in the background along with a line of nations' flags. It's a powerful image, whereas the 'Aces High' sleeve showing Eddie in a fighter plane cockpit is much simpler. The Riggs logo is again present on all of these. It is just above the pyramid entrance on the album and below and to the left of Eddie on both of the single sleeves.

'Aces High' (Harris)

Another great album-opener, this storming rocker from the pen of Harris takes its lyrical theme from the point of view of a British fighter pilot in the air during the Battle of Britain, 1940 – a three-month heroic defensive action against the might of the German Luftwaffe, which in total cost the RAF 792 planes and the Luftwaffe 1,389. The lyric is short and succinct, yet gets its point over brilliantly, as it conjures up the desperate cat-and-mouse manoeuvring of the opposing aircraft, enhanced by the breathless, continued attack of the music. The ME 109 referred to in the lyric is the German Messerschmitt BF 109 – probably the most powerful fighter plane in the world at that time, yet beaten for quick evasive action by the faster turning British Spitfires and Hurricanes.

The track begins with a mid-paced intro, powerful yet clearly serving as an appetiser for the main course. This duly arrives very shortly with a lightning-paced guitar and bass-driven riff which never lets up – no nice melodic interludes here, just as there would be no such thing in battle over Southern England. After each verse (there are only two), there is a gripping pre-chorus ('Rolling, turning, diving...') before the big, typically Maiden chorus proper arrives with Dickinson taking flight himself on the 'Live to fly, fly to live' section. As a live song, and indeed as an album opener, it's hard to beat for excitement.

The song was released as a single (Number 20 in the UK), and as such there was an official video for it. Following the Maiden tradition of mixing live performance with archive film footage, in this case, there are dramatic black and white combat visuals working superbly with the live footage, which itself illustrates how powerful the song would be in the live environment. The track is preceded by Winston Churchill's 'Their Finest Hour' speech, as it would regularly be when opening live shows. Astonishingly, Nicko McBrain appears to have aged about 20 years since *Piece of Mind*, having gone from the unfeasibly fresh-faced youth in the videos from that album to suddenly looking like the Nicko we all know in this one. Perhaps he'd had a lot of worries...

One thing about 'Aces High' which is something of a peculiarity is that the song structure is an almost perfect mirror, revolving around the point between the guitar solos when Murray hands over to Smith. The song begins with the introduction; then there is a fast guitar harmony section, the verse and chorus, a 16-bar section in A minor then a 16-bar solo. At this point, the song reverses and we have a sort of musical palindrome, with another 16-bar solo, followed by 16-bars in A minor, verse/chorus, identical fast guitar section and finally the climactic cadenza (the 'big finish', if you like). If you ignore the fact that the introduction is at the start and the cadenza at the end, the rest of the song is a mirror effect, with almost mathematical precision.

'2 Minutes to Midnight' (Smith, Dickinson)
The first single from the album (Number Eleven in the UK chart), this protest song about the politics of war and destruction, particularly from a nuclear point of view, remains one of Maiden's most recognisable songs to the world at large. The title comes from the 'Doomsday Clock', a device introduced in the late 1940s to represent how close the world is to the brink of annihilation. In 1953, the clock was moved to 'two minutes to midnight', the nearest it has ever been. In 1972 the clock had recovered back to seven minutes, while in 1984 when this song came out, it stood at three minutes to. A few years ago, progress had been made in the scenario of world peace, with the result that the minute hand was put back again to seven minutes. However, following US/Korean discord, and also the looming spectre of climate change joining the feast, January 2018 saw the time set to two minutes to midnight once again, for the first time since 1953.

The song itself is nothing short of brilliant, an almost perfect mix of classic, meaningful rock music and a chorus which burrows its way into your brain. It crashes along on what seems at first to be just another galloping Maiden assault, but as the pre-chorus arrives it switches on a dime to exactly half-tempo, and focuses the ear in sharp relief, before the 'Two minutes to midnight' line is spat out with venom by Dickinson as the tempo redoubles at the perfect moment. The lyric, illustrating the folly and corruption of the war machine, demonstrates again that Dickinson, while often overlooked as such, is Maiden's finest wordsmith on his day. Lines such as 'The body bags and little rags of children torn in two', 'A prime-time Belsen feast' and 'To the tune of starving millions, to make a better kind of gun' hit home powerfully. And in a subversive kind of a way, it probably left millions of *Top of the Pops* watchers unconsciously singing along in their heads with 'Two minutes to midnight / To kill the unborn in the womb', which didn't happen with the charts every week!

Again, there was an official video, following the 'live with interspersed film footage' pattern, this time showing scenes of mysterious cabals, shady businessmen dealing with armed thugs, a politician watching it all on TV from behind his desk and men typing away on computer terminals with hieroglyphics on the keys, with 'Eye of Horus' symbols on their immaculate shirt cuffs. All very deep and meaningful!

'Losfer Words (Big 'Orra)' (Harris)

As might be guessed from the title ('Lost for words'), this is an instrumental – the fourth and last one that the band would record – up to the time of writing at least. Musically, there isn't really too much to say about it, as it has some nice guitar harmonies and some great bass playing for sure, with Smith pulling off a good solo, but it ultimately fails to hold the attention. The major difference between this and 'Genghis Khan' and 'Transylvania' is that, whereas those two songs were originally intended to have lyrics but were left because they sounded so good without them, this one is very much the opposite. It has no lyrics yet it sounds as if it should. It sounds rather like a karaoke version of a track with the vocals removed – there is something missing. A Dickinson-shaped hole, effectively. It canters along powerfully and has some very good moments, but all in all, it's just a bit empty. It's a bit like fish and chips without salt or vinegar.

The subtitle 'Big 'Orra' is rather strange. On the face of it, it is simply a cockney way of saying 'Big Horror', but that doesn't really make any sense itself, unless Harris was giving his own critique of the track! It could be a pun on the Irish exclamation 'Begorrah!', meaning 'By God!', but that doesn't make a lot more sense either. Anyhow, the band must have liked it as it made its way into the live set for the tour. Maybe it was intended to give Bruce a rest!

'Flash of the Blade' (Dickinson)

Bruce Dickinson's love of fencing comes to the fore in this somewhat slight tale of a young boy learning to fight with a wooden sword who grows up to fight for real as he avenges his murdered family (at least, we assume it to be his family making up the 'house of smoking ruins and the bodies at your feet'). It's not one of his deepest or most profound lyrics, but then again it is clearly intended more as a *Boys' Own Paper* tale of derring-do, and in that regard, it works well.

Musically, it is similarly basic. A nice hammer-on guitar intro gives way to a fast driving rocker of the sort that Maiden could probably do in their sleep by now, with a suitably anthemic chorus which calls to mind Errol Flynn crashing in through a window and swinging on the chandelier, as the bad guys go down under his blade. It is all very enjoyable in a testosterone-pumping, *Ripping Yarns* sort of a way, but ultimately without too much substance. There is an instrumental section, but no guitar solo as such. The track has never been played live, and that is understandable, really.

'The Duellists' (Harris)
More fencing action here, this time centring on a duel between two men. In fact, Harris was inspired by a 1978 film of the same name, directed by Ridley Scott – itself based on a 1908 Joseph Conrad novel entitled *The Duel* – about two rival French officers during the Napoleonic period and the lifelong feud which consumes them. The lyric eschews any of the overall plot in favour of a look at one particular – and fatal – duel. Dickinson goes about his task with gusto, clearly relishing this sort of subject matter, and his voice soars satisfyingly during the 'Oh, oh – fight for the honour' chorus.

The verses chug along powerfully, building up to that slightly by-the-numbers anthemic chorus, but more than half of the song's six-minute length is taken up by an extended instrumental mid-section. With a number of changes keeping the interest and excitement up, and two excellent guitar solos by Murray and then Smith, it is, in fact, this mid-section which contains the song's truly great moments. A perfect example of a merely good song turned into something more in the hands of a great band, it has perhaps surprisingly never been performed live. It certainly sees off the first side in fine fashion, after a slight dip in quality with the previous two tracks.

'Back in the Village' (Smith, Dickinson)
In which the inspirational source of the TV show *The Prisoner* is mined once again, after the Harris song on *The Number of the Beast* album. This time with Dickinson is at the lyrical helm. Clearly a fan, Bruce makes the track far more true to the show than the earlier Harris allegorical effort, as several catch-phrases and quotations from the show are woven into the lyric, although the additional references to dropping bombs and waving white flags seems to be taking a generalised anti-war stance. It may be that he is comparing the Prisoner's situation in the village with people stuck in a wartime scenario – but there is certainly some evocative imagery, and the TV references such as 'Questions are a burden and answers a prison for oneself' are fun for aficionados, for sure. The line 'paper cats and burning barns' has been the subject of much speculation over the years, with no definitive answer as to what a paper cat actually is. It may well be something invented by Dickinson as an interesting image, as searching for true meanings come up short. It does mean a coward in an expression of Iraqi origin, but even with the unpredictable Bruce, it seems unlikely for Iraqi colloquialisms to have been plundered for inspiration. A 'paper cat' is also, as it happens, the name of a

47

'masturbation device' (yes, 'device') designed by the Marquis de Sade, but I think we can all profoundly hope that has no connection.

Musically, this gets a lot of criticism among Maiden fans, who regularly single out the chorus for their disapproval. True, it isn't exactly the most uplifting Maiden chorus ever, but it's short and to the point, and the guitar riff driving the song along is truly superb, as are Murray and Smith's solos, and overall it works pretty well. Murray again takes the first solo before Smith – it is interesting to note just how often they do the solos in that particular order and makes one wonder whether it is a personal preference on the part of one or both of them to go first or second...

'Powerslave' (Dickinson)

Ah, now here is where things get undeniably classic, and the point where all of the Egyptian iconographies of the cover art finally makes sense. The lyrics are from the point of view of an Egyptian Pharaoh at the time of his death, lamenting the limits of his power here on earth. He was a God, he reasons, so why can he not live forever? In the end, he has, he realises become a 'slave to the power of death'.

The track is classic Maiden, there is no doubt. The riff driving the verses is powerful and almost metronomic in its brutalising repetition. This gives way to a grand spiralling of the music before the big, epic chorus has the Pharaoh crying out 'Tell me why I had to be a Powerslave!' All this has a subtly Egyptian sound to it, lending just the right air of exotica and menace. There is a lengthy instrumental section, containing no less than three guitar solos. Murray opens things with a slow, measured and beautifully expressive solo over a subdued backing until the tempo kicks up again and he delivers another solo, this time in the more usual Maiden fret-blazing fashion. Harris gets in on the action himself with a short passage spotlighting his nimble and dextrous bass playing, before Smith storms in with a massive solo of slashing intensity which is probably the pick of the bunch. Back to that sledgehammer opening riff again, another chorus and a big finish – and we're done just over the seven-minute mark.

As one would expect from Dickinson the Human Encyclopedia, there are several lyrical references which are worth looking at. The Eye of Horus was a powerful sign in Egyptian superstition, said to ward off evil and provide protection. Seen on the album cover, it resembles a line drawing of an eye but actually consists of six separate symbols, each representing one of the senses as the Egyptians saw them, in descending order of their perceived importance: smell, sight, thought, hearing, taste, touch. Horus was the son of Osiris, who fought to avenge his father when he was slain by his own brother, Set. Horus won the battle but lost an eye in the process. This was restored by Thoth, allowing Horus, in turn, to restore Osiris to life. This is the source of the legend of the Eye, and is referred to in the line 'Enter the risen Osiris – risen again'. Osiris can also be interpreted to be the equivalent of our modern-day 'Reaper' image, appearing at the point of death.

The final verse goes on to the point when the Pharaoh's tomb may be breached long, long afterwards, and plays on the 'Curse' legend propagated after the tomb of Tutankhamun was opened by Howard Carter in 1922. In fact, newspaper reports at the time were luridly sensational, with several going as far as to invent non-existent dire warnings supposedly written inside the burial chamber, and despite some reports of up to 26 people perishing in mysterious circumstances during the decade following the opening of the tomb, this, in fact, was only six, with one guard who actually slept in the burial chamber passing away in 1980 at the ripe old age of 81! The world was very receptive to these tales a century ago as, throughout the 1800s, there had been a brisk supply of books containing terrifying tales of cursed tombs and ambulatory mummies. A curse was far more interesting than the more prosaic explanations such as mould spores and other disease-carrying things being disturbed.

It's a good song, though!

'The Rime of the Ancient Mariner' (Harris)

The real *piece de resistance* closes the album and gives Harris another chance to explore his extremely well-read literary leanings. *The Rime of the Ancient Mariner* is, of course, an epic poem by Samuel Taylor Coleridge, and one highly familiar to generations of beleaguered schoolchildren who have been tasked with studying it. Harris takes up the challenge of telling the story of this huge work within thirteen-and-a-half minutes of spellbinding heavy rock music. It's a long way from 'All Shook Up', for sure...

It has to be said, although I have admittedly voiced the occasional criticism of Harris's lyrics, he does an incredible job here of summarising a 77-page book into an easily digestible lyric. Not only that, but he hits all of the salient points and also references the allegorical meanings of the work. A schoolboy could practically write an essay on the work simply by listening to this. Quite brilliant!

Musically, it managed to match up to the quality of the lyrics with ease, as it seems to fly by in a fraction of its considerable length. A magnificent Maiden 'gallop' propels the spine of the song, while the vocal melody has just the right amount of ebb and flow to prevent it ever becoming repetitive. The chorus ('And the ship sailed on and on and North at sea', etc.) is one of the very best Dickinson ever delivered, and indeed he is absolutely key to the success of the piece, getting inside the lyric and delivering it with the skill and nuance of a master storyteller. At the five-minute mark, things slow right down to a reflective passage, all creaking timbers and ambient sea sounds, as four lines of the poem are directly quoted via spoken word. This is the second such direct citation from the poem itself, as four lines are actually put to music and sung perfectly a little earlier (including the most famous – and often misquoted – line 'water, water everywhere, nor any drop to drink'). After the quiet passage, the heavy instrumental section comes in with Smith this time taking the first solo as both men play out of their skins.

There are many contenders for the greatest Maiden song. And all have their meritorious claims. But there can be no discussion of that subject without this masterpiece at least being thrown into the mix. Single-handedly it takes a strong album and elevates it to the status of an undoubted classic. Remember, this was only four years since 'Phantom of the Opera' was lauded for its scope, depth and ambition, on an album which also included 'Running Free'. That's progress and development on a Beatles '62 to'66 level, and yet something for which Maiden rarely receive plaudits.

Related songs:
'Rainbow's Gold' (Slesser, Mountain)
The B-side of the '2 Minutes to Midnight' single, this song is actually a cover of a track by obscure 1970s prog band Beckett. Its presence is partially explained by Nicko McBrain, who claimed that members of Maiden and Beckett had been friends. The writers of the song were Terry Slesser and Kenny Mountain; Slesser is best known for his time in Paul Kossoff's band Back Street Crawler, later rechristened Crawler after Kossoff's demise. Maiden manager Rod Smallwood was also Beckett's agent before he met Maiden.

The Maiden version is, unsurprisingly, much heavier than the original, but it is still far from being a classic. It underlines how much better Bruce has always sounded when tackling a song written with him in mind – this one is lacking in vocal melody, and he struggles to impose himself on it.

There is, in fact, a second B-side to this single, though rather than a song, it consists of a secretly recorded (by Dickinson) argument between Harris and Nicko when a message, delivered via a roadie after the bass had problems and a drum solo was to be extended, was misunderstood. Titled 'Mission From 'Arry', it doesn't repay too many repeated listening, but should be heard at least once!

'King of Twilight' (Nektar)
In which Maiden highlight their prog-rock influences yet again, with this cover of a song by British band Nektar from their 1972 *A Tab in the Ocean* album. In fact, it is a mix of two songs from that album, 'Crying in The Dark' and 'King of Twilight' itself. It's good, and an interesting twist on the original for sure, but it's unlikely that few Nektar fans would see it as an improvement. It has to be said though, that giving some lesser-known bands of that ilk an introduction to a potential new audience was an exceptionally good thing to do, and the band (and probably Harris in particular) deserve great credit.

Somewhere in Time

Personnel:
Bruce Dickinson: vocals
Dave Murray: guitars, guitar synthesizer
Adrian Smith: guitars, guitar synthesizer, backing vocals
Steve Harris: bass guitar, bass synthesizer
Nicko McBrain: drums
Record Label: EMI (UK), Capitol (US)
Recorded:1986, produced by Martin Birch
Release date: 29 September 1986
Highest chart places: UK: 3, USA: 11
Running time: 51:18

When Maiden finally came off the massive World Slavery tour, they were mentally and physically burned out. As a result of this, immediately following the tour they all took four months off to get themselves back into the game again. Smith, Harris and Murray spent much of that time experimenting with new equipment, notably guitar synthesizers, while Bruce Dickinson began thinking ahead to how he saw the next record in his head and coming up with songs to reflect that. Essentially, he believed that they had to shake things up and come from a new direction in order to keep things fresh for yet another year-long tour, but his radical, largely acoustic-based material was rejected by the band – leading to him having no writing credits at all on the resulting album. As he put it himself, 'I felt we had to come up with our *Physical Graffiti* or *Led Zeppelin IV* ... we had to get it onto another level, or we'd stagnate and drift away'. Harris, in particular, believed no such thing and felt that the stress of the tour had caused the singer to 'lose the plot' somewhat.

That was far from the only contentious thing about the material for the record, however, as it was adorned with guitar synths on almost every song – though it must be stressed, not to an especially intrusive degree. Still, this departure from the perceived 'purity' of Maiden as a guitar band did cause its share of controversy among fans. However, the strength of the songs won out, and the album is today regarded among the very best of Maiden's output.

If Dickinson was out of the writing picture this time around, Harris was not left to shoulder the burden alone. Adrian Smith stepped up to the plate in grand style, composing three songs entirely on his own, the other songs being made up of four from Harris and one Harris / Murray collaboration.

Recording again took place at Compass Point in Nassau, but this time not all of it, as the expensive recording process saw the bass and drums alone recorded there, with the guitars and vocals done in Wisseloord Studios in The Netherlands. The mixing took place in New York. This does appear to be in stark contrast to the 'all for one' attitude Maiden had always appeared to espouse, but it was ultimately successful. The album again reached the Top Five in the UK, this time peaking at Number Three, while in America it would improve on its predecessor and reach Number Eleven. Clearly, the two-year break since *Powerslave* had not had any detrimental effect, but then again 1985 had seen the release of the massively successful live double album *Live After Death*, so Maiden had not travelled far from the public consciousness.

Album Cover:

Well, where do we start with this one? There are so many hidden references on this cover that it is very tricky, yet fascinating, to spot them all. The artwork forms a wraparound picture depicting a half-cyborg looking Eddie in a futuristic city, something like a cross between *Judge Dredd* and *Blade Runner*. Scandalously, however, it was not originally issued in the gatefold sleeve it was crying out for (except for, oddly, the Peruvian release, which had the inner sleeve artwork on the inner gatefold). By 1986, it was becoming ever more difficult to get albums released in the more expensive gatefold format, and Maiden was suffering for this like many of their contemporaries. The inner sleeve had a band photo on one side and lyrics on the other.

To list all of the hidden references in the artwork would be a lengthy job, but some of them are as follows: Firstly, on the front cover, there are nods to previous albums, such as a street sign reading 'Acacia', a neon Eye of Horus and a litter bin identical to the one on the first album. A sign reading 'Websters' is a reference to EMI's artistic director Charlie Webster. A neon-lit Russian phrase translates, for some reason, as 'I'm vomiting', while a banner can be made out which reads 'This is a very boring painting'. It took Riggs three months to complete it, so I imagine to him, it really was a boring painting by the end...

Things continue on the reverse, with two obvious references being a digital clock reading 23:58 (two minutes to midnight), and a sign reading 'Long Beach Arena', which is where much of *Live After Death* was recorded. Below the clock, a sign reads 'Phantom Opera House', while below that reads 'Bollocks again and again'! There are signs for the 'Ancient Mariner Seafood Restaurant', 'Upton Park' (where West Ham United played at the time), the 'Sand Dune' bar and favourite Maiden London venues the Marquee Club and Rainbow, while their old stomping ground The Ruskin Arms is also shown. A scoreboard displays West Ham beating Arsenal 7-3, in an enormous moment of optimism. The 'Herbert Ails' sign is a cheeky reference to the demise of their nemesis, author Frank Herbert, the previous year.

Elsewhere, other locations nodded to are 'Tehe's Bar' (where vocals on 'Wasted Years' were recorded), 'Hammerjacks' (a Baltimore club frequented by the band) and 'L'Amours', a New York venue. Another Russian sign translates as, bizarrely, 'yoghurt', while there is also a rather hard to read sign at the bottom which reads 'Sanctuary Music Shop' – it's just next to a small EMI sign. A prominent Japanese phrase alludes to a respected philosopher named Akira Asada, which points very strongly to Dickinson. The bracket holding Eddie's skull together after his lobotomy is carved into the wall, while just above that, for some reason, stands Batman. There are quite a few more, so try spotting them – including several references to *Blade Runner*, as a nod to the artwork inspiration.

Shrinking the artwork to CD size really spoiled this sort of thing, and how on earth it is supposed to work on an iPod thumbnail is anyone's guess, but such is progress, I suppose.

'Caught Somewhere in Time' (Harris)

The guitar synths are noticeable in the introduction to this Harris song, but they do sound good, and also pretty much disappear as the song gets into its stride. One would think from the cover art and the title that this would be some kind of futuristic / time-travel yarn, but it appears to be a story about a man being tempted to sell his soul – though for what exactly, we don't know. It's a decent enough lyric, but far from one of his literary masterpieces.

Musically – yeah, it's pretty good. It hurtles along at a rattling pace, and the instrumental section (with Smith again saying a virtual 'after you, sir', as Murray takes the first solo) is sublime, with the momentum absolutely thrilling, like a runaway train that could hurtle off the rails at any moment. The chorus is the only thing which takes it down a small notch, with Dickinson sounding a little uncomfortable and forced as he warbles the word 'time'. It's also very repetitive. Fortunately, the rest of the song makes up for it, so we'll give them a pass! The line 'Just let yourself go', with the vocal effect on the final word, is rather reminiscent of Rainbow's epic 'A Light in the Black', which can never, ever be a bad thing.

At almost seven-and-a-half minutes, this was the longest opening track on a Maiden album until 'Sign of the Cross' on *The X Factor*, and the longest on a Dickinson-fronted album until *The Final Frontier* in 2010. It works, though, and doesn't really outstay its welcome.

'Wasted Years' (Smith)

The first single from the album, this was actually released a short time before the parent album came out. This accounts for the cover of the single itself, showing a time machine control panel with only Eddie's head visible as a reflection. This, according to Riggs, was because the album cover had not yet been previewed, and they didn't want to give away Eddie's new 'cyborg' guise. As a result, the cover really bears very little relevance to the lyric. It also features the Tardis, from *Doctor Who*, which may explain its small depiction on the back of the album cover.

The lyric has two thrusts to it by all appearances. The clear message of the uplifting chorus is to live for today and not waste time looking back, whether in regret or pointless nostalgia. However, the verses seem to have clear references to the wearisome effects of the long, gruelling World Slavery tour, and the feelings of homesickness and loneliness it caused. Overall, it's a very accomplished lyric and matched by the music which is one of Maiden's finest ever marriages of mainstream appeal with the classic Maiden sound, up there

with 'Run to the Hills' and '2 Minutes to Midnight'.
Disappointingly, it only reached Number 18 in the UK singles chart, when it really deserved much better. Smith takes the solo himself, which is perhaps unsurprising as he wrote the song. Note that this is the only track on the album to feature no guitar synthesizers at all. Old-school Maiden at its finest.

There was an official video for the single, which sees the band performing the song in monochrome footage in a studio in Germany, interspersed with clips from previous Maiden single videos and also lots of still photos of the band out and about on the *World Slavery* tour. There was also an amusing incident on a German TV show when the band swapped instruments onstage, in humorous protest at the amount of miming work they were having to do!

'Sea of Madness' (Smith)

Once again Smith delivers the goods with this lyrically oblique song. It's a lyric which has had a fair number of sometimes fanciful ideas attributed to it, such as it being about the moment when the soul leaves the body after an accident, or even to do with the Normandy beach landings in World War II. It's hard to divine the full meaning, but at its simplest level, it seems to be someone deciding that mankind is going 'to hell in a handbasket' and electing to 'opt-out'. In truth, it's not the greatest song on the album. Opening with a massively propulsive, percussive riff which it maintains through the verses, it's a little like a heavier and more 'industrial' version of Deep Purple's 'You Fool No One' from their *Burn* album. Smith again hogs the spotlight, contributing the superb guitar solo in the track.

'Heaven Can Wait' (Harris)

Another Harris song to close the first side of vinyl, this song is about someone caught between life and death, at that 'tunnel and white light' moment so often described by people claiming to have witnessed it. It seems to be quite a highly regarded song by a big portion of the fanbase and remained in the setlist for some time, but to these ears, it's one of the weaker points on the album. The band are tight as usual, and Murray and Smith (the latter after the 'oh-oh-oh' section) both pull off great solos, but being honest, there's not much of a song here. The verses are fast but not particularly memorable, and the chorus is irritating and repetitive.

The aforementioned 'oh-oh-oh' section sees the band roping in a group of people (from an establishment called Tehe's Bar – hence the sign on the cover) to deliver a series of 'oh-oh-oh' vocals which are so obviously planned as audience participation that it hurts. Come on guys, you're better than this. 'Ancient Mariner' didn't need a gang of rent-a-choir guys bellowing 'oh, oh, he's an ancient sailor' to get its point across. At over seven minutes, it's stretched out tighter than Nicko's drum skins, and it outstays its welcome a couple of minutes before the end.

'The Loneliness of the Long Distance Runner' (Harris)

Back to literary inspiration for this Harris song, inspired by a short story by Alan Sillitoe, which was made into a 1962 film of the same title. The book concerns a boy from a poor upbringing sentenced to borstal (young offenders' prison) for the petty crime into which he has fallen. A gifted runner, he is selected to run a prestigious cross country race representing the prison, with a promise of light duties for the remaining six months of his sentence if he wins. On the day of the race, however, he reflects as he runs on whether he actually wants to win in order to gain honour for the institution at the price of his own dignity, and he decides to throw the race. Way ahead of the pack, he stops just before the finish line and lets himself be overtaken. Even though he is back to hard labour, he never regrets his decision.

As much about the runner as a metaphor for personal choice and freedom as it is about the actual plot, the story is a typical one to pique Harris's compositional interest, though his lyric is more about the race itself, with few allusions to the actual dilemma, and it doesn't reveal him finally choosing to lose. In some ways that is a good decision, as people who are not familiar with the book or film can take their own personal inspiration and interpretation from it, but it also makes it seem a little unfinished.

In fact, at least half of the six-and-a-half-minute track is instrumental, which in this case is a good thing. Not because Dickinson's performance is lacking – indeed he is excellent here – but more because the vocal melody and the chorus simply aren't that good. Far better is the mid-song instrumental, lasting for some time before a short interim 'verse' leads into the guitar solo, this time led off by Smith. This is a perfect illustration of the fact that Maiden was such a great band by this time that they could always lift material to greater heights, even when the song itself was lacking. As such, it is enjoyable but not essential Maiden. The song opens with a strident guitar theme which is oddly enough extremely reminiscent of the song 'It's a Sin' by the Pet Shop Boys, although, in fact, that is the other way around, with the latter song not appearing until a year later, and was itself accused of plagiarising 'Wild World' by Cat Stevens. The world of 1980s music was a knotty place indeed!

It has been said quite often by people that they find this song quite exhausting to listen to. This is almost certainly caused by the fact that Nicko's drumming appears deliberately to be timed to simulate the actual pace of a runner's footsteps. Once you hear it, it seems even more tiring. In the hands of a lesser drummer, you would put it down to coincidence, but with Nicko, you feel sure it is deliberate.

'Stranger in a Strange Land' (Smith)

Based on Maiden's history of songwriting inspiration, one would assume this to be based on the science fiction book by Robert Heinlein, but it is entirely unrelated – of course, it is Harris who most favours the direct literary constructs, and this is written by Adrian Smith. The subject matter actually refers to a member of a polar expedition who gets lost and whose preserved frozen body is found years later by another group of explorers. Smith got the idea when he met a man who had himself encountered a frozen body in this exact same way, and it left a deep impression on him. That worked both ways as it happened because the explorer himself became a fan of the band through his association with them.

The second single from the album, it only reached Number 22 on the UK charts and isn't quite as strong as 'Wasted Years', but that isn't to say it isn't a very good song in its own right. Very much on the more commercial edge of Maiden's repertoire, it has a strong melody throughout and is popular with most fans despite its 'poppier' sheen. The cover art is very misleading, furthering the impression that there would be a Heinlein connection. Smith once again takes both guitar solos (a fast one, but even a slower one before it, which would normally be very much Murray's domain). He liked to play the solos on his own material, it would appear.

Note that there was an official video for the single, but on this occasion, it is a straightforward performance with no intercut sequences or storytelling. It is also responsible for an outrageous codpiece sported by Bruce Dickinson, along with leather pants and a billowing pirate shirt which actually manage to direct attention away from the fact that Harris is resplendent in Spandex pants with one blue leg and one white leg. Smith, modelling a bullet belt and spandex combination, seems almost under-dressed. The '80s have a lot to answer for.

'Déjà Vu' (Harris, Murray)
This is a lyrically very simple song, with lyrics concerning the feeling you have when you have witnessed something before. It is a lyrically very simple song, with... sorry, you knew I was going to do that!

Harris seems to be deliberately taking a more direct and stripped back lyrical approach, as even without any historical or literary target to aim for, he could easily have waxed, well, lyrical, about the possible causes and psychological reasons behind the phenomenon, but he lets the music do the talking, which works well. The song has no pretence but hurtles along in a headlong fashion while also having some nice melodic touches for Bruce to get his larynx around. It's a rare songwriting outing for Dave Murray, but he does seem to have a habit of contributing to good ones. Other than a short, laid-back opening solo from Murray, there are no solos in this one, with twin lead lines carrying the day.

'Alexander the Great' (Harris)
Ah, you knew he hadn't left his history books at home when he went into the studio, didn't you? Harris gets back to his scholarly best with this treatise about the life and legacy of Alexander of Macedon, the military genius from the 4th Century BC who conquered the Persian Empire and reportedly never lost a single battle. It even opens with a quote from King Philip of Macedonia, circa

349BC. Take THAT, any other metal band with intellectual aspirations! I mean, it may be that Steve Harris was a hard lovin' man who liked to rock and roll all night, but he sure didn't like to talk about it if so...

There is no attempt to look at Alexander from any metaphorical or interpretive angle in this song – it is no less than the history of his military achievements laid out in text-book form, which makes it a remarkable approach to a metal song, even by Maiden standards. The lyric has come in for criticism from scholars and enthusiasts hung up on the historical accuracy, but this is unfair to my way of thinking. It is true that the claim near the end that his army refused to follow him into India is blatantly false, as they fought with him right down as far as the Indus river. Likewise, we could dispute the timeline of such events as the cutting of the Gordian Knot, which is widely agreed not to have happened – as the legend has it – in any case. However, such complaints ignore the fact that this is a song lyric, not a historical tome, and that getting the factual reportage of the lyric to scan and be sung as it is, takes a lot of skill. There are many great and learned historians who have written extraordinary works examining the minutiae of Alexander's life and deeds, but one suspects that these great men might come unstuck if presented with a pen and paper by Bruce Dickinson with a request to 'summarise this in around twenty lines so I can deliver it as a heavy rock song please'.

Musically, the eight-and-a-half minutes here serve to utterly confound the expectations of the listener. A mellow opening section, lasting well over a minute, has Smith again taking a kind of solo atypical of him over a martial drumbeat reminiscent of that in Ravel's 'Bolero', for example. When, as we approach the two-minute mark, a familiar Maiden gallop comes in, the listener feels secure and on familiar ground, but that particular rug is pulled out from underneath when the central instrumental section begins towards the four-minute mark. The first guitar solo, again from Smith, is over a 7/8 musical backdrop, utterly throwing the listener's musical compass off, and this lengthy, meandering section continues through a series of changing time signatures, with some bass licks from Harris which emerge from the musical 'fog' to throw one's ears off course again and again. It's so unlike Maiden that it can surely only have been a deliberate statement, perhaps as a riposte to those who claimed Maiden songs all sounded predictably similar. Murray finally gets a solo here at 6:30, but it is a good one.

When the final verse comes in, the musical curveballs aren't over, with the number of notes and words increased to give the feel of more and more momentum, and leaving the listener feeling as exhausted as the battle-weary armies being described. Perhaps the only real criticism to be laid is that the end is something of a whimper rather than a bang. The final line 'Alexander the Great / He died of fever in Babylon' seems to appear from nowhere, and the song and story just... finish. Ironically, this is one instance when the oft-criticised Maiden habit of endlessly repeating choruses fails to happen at all, on an occasion when it might well have served the song better. Leaving that aside, however, this is an extraordinary album closer. The fever at the end is believed to have been malaria, incidentally.

Related songs:
'Reach Out' (Colwell)
The B-side to the 'Wasted Years' single, some background information is required to put this unlikely-sounding track into context. After the end of the World Slavery tour, while the band took six months off, Nicko began getting itchy musical feet and rented a studio inviting Adrian Smith to come and jam with him, to keep his hand in, so to speak. Smith brought along some friends, including members of the melodic rock band FM, and they played and also wrote a few songs, including this one. The whole thing ended up leading to a one-off show under the banner of The Entire Population of Hackney, at which Smith, Murray and Dickinson also appeared for the encore. This song was written by Dave 'Bucket' Colwell, an early member of FM and later to do time as guitarist in a post-millennial line-up of Bad Company. FM also recorded a version, but substantially reworked. A second gig by the collective followed, but this time under the name The Sherman Tankers. Ah, Nicko...

Musically, the track is a pleasant but unremarkable AOR song, sounding more like Bryan Adams than Iron Maiden, with this unfamiliarity being compounded by Smith handling lead vocals. Bruce joins in on the chorus, but it remains the only recorded Maiden song not to have lead vocals by the current singer.

'Sheriff of Huddersfield' (Iron Maiden)
If 'Reach Out' was an unlikely song, this second track on the B-side of the 12" single was frankly bizarre! The Sheriff of the title was Maiden manager Rod Smallwood, a native of Huddersfield who had moved to Los Angeles and was missing a lot of things about England, such as rugby, cricket, Yorkshire beer and mushy peas, and he scarcely missed an opportunity to complain about it. According to Nicko, the last straw was when he paid a fortune for an enormous satellite dish to get English programmes on, only to find that all it allowed him to get was South American TV!

The band wrote the song as a hilarious tribute to his complaining, with Dickinson adding a sort of running commentary in Smallwood's broad Yorkshire accent. Knowing he would probably block it, they kept the song a closely guarded secret until it was released, so the first Rod heard of it was on the single itself. It's an entertaining song, but certainly not to be taken as anything other than the very funny piece that it is. Anyhow, Rod seemed to learn his lesson, as he apparently returned not too long afterwards.

'That Girl' (Barnett, Goldsworth, Jupp)
Another refugee from the Entire Population of Hackney project, this 'Stranger in a Strange Land' B-side was one of the demo tracks recorded by FM in 1986

and which got them their record deal. They later re-recorded it in 1986 with their then-current line-up. Lyrically it is totally un-Maiden-like, being a fairly straightforward love song, but Dickinson works his vocal magic on it, giving it enough of a Maiden stamp to make it fit better than 'Reach Out'. Nicko McBrain claimed that these tracks were all recorded by him and Smith alone (with Bruce on vocals), but that is clearly untrue in this case as Dave Murray provides the first guitar solo here, and also the solo on 'Reach Out'. It's better than the FM version, to these ears. An underrated track.

Andy Barnett, who co-wrote the song, was in Smith's pre-Maiden band Urchin, and would also join him in his ASAP project during his later time away from Maiden.

'Juanita' (Barnacle, O'Neill)
The third Hackney-related song, appearing on the 'Stranger...' 12" single, this one was originally played by one of Andy Barnett's bands, Marshall Fury, though they never recorded it. Again, it's not bad, though not as good as 'That Girl'. It is possible that this track could have been recorded without Harris and Murray, as there is certainly no evidence of Murray anywhere on this one, and despite Dickinson's vocals, it doesn't sound very much like Maiden at all.

Lyrically it's a bit odd, with the man in the song proclaiming in the verses that he has to get his girl – Juanita – back, whatever it takes, but then in the chorus vowing that he is never going back. In the final choruses Dickinson, indicating that the song was not being taken 100% seriously, changes the words from the original 'I'm never going back Juanita' to 'I'm never going down on Juanita'!

Seventh Son of a Seventh Son

Personnel:
Bruce Dickinson: vocals
Dave Murray: guitars
Adrian Smith: guitars, synthesizer
Steve Harris: bass guitar, string synthesizer
Nicko McBrain: drums
Record Label: EMI (UK), Capitol (US)
Recorded: Feb-March 1988, produced by Martin Birch
Release date: 11 April 1988
Highest chart places: UK: 1, USA: 12
Running time: 43:51

The first Maiden album to have a real unifying concept behind it, the idea for *Seventh Son...* came from Harris, unsurprisingly enough. It was to be their seventh studio album, and he was searching for ideas until he happened to read the novel *Seventh Son* by fantasy/sci-fi writer Orson Scott Card. This book told the story of a seventh son of a seventh son who possesses all sorts of powers. He liked the idea as a title for the seventh album, but after a phone call to Bruce Dickinson the pair had become enthused about the idea of a concept, and it grew from there. All of the songs were written with the concept of the seventh son and his powers in mind, though the album as a whole didn't exactly have a complete story arc to it – the second side does have a thread running through it from the birth to the death of the seventh son, but the first four songs are more difficult to make a plot out of. They can be shoehorned in (and I will get that particular shoehorn into use when discussing the individual songs) but are perhaps best thought of as fitting the theme, and the idea of the mystical seventh son concept. Certainly, Dickinson looked back on the album later and expressed his regret that they didn't go further in coming up with a proper narrative thread running through the album, but Harris has always seemed satisfied with the lyrical approach.

The album moved on a step from the guitar synths of *Somewhere in Time* by being the first Maiden album to use actual keyboards, in the form of traditional synthesizers, although they decided not to hire a keyboard player as, according to Dickinson, it was 'mostly one finger stuff', handled by Smith and Harris. On the resulting tour, bass tech Michael Kenney handled the keyboards, performing the title song in black cape and mask, under the guise of 'The Count'. Harris was very pleased with the album, singling out its more progressive nature as a strong reason why he thought it their 'best since *Piece of Mind*', but although it topped the charts in the UK (the first to do so since *The Number of the Beast*) it sold relatively poorly in America, a fact which dismayed him. It still reached Number Twelve in the US, however – one place lower than the previous album and higher than *Powerslave* – so its performance was, in fact, fairly consistent with the band's profile over there.

Recording for this album took place in the new surroundings of Musicland Studios in Germany, previously used by such bands as Rainbow on several occasions, and was completed relatively quickly considering the nature of the material, with recording commencing in February 1988 and the album in the shops by 11 April. It was to be the last album with the line-up which had stayed together since *Piece of Mind*, as Adrian Smith would leave after this one, but that is a story for the next album. For the moment, the line-up was stable, there was much more co-writing than on the previous album (with Dickinson back in the writing fold), and all was right with the Maiden World.

Album Cover:

If the progressive nature of the album and the inclusion of keyboards divided some fans, the Riggs cover art did so even further, with many fans to this day proclaiming it to be either the best or the worst cover art up to this point. It's certainly much more simplistic than the grand artistic endeavours of *Powerslave* and *Somewhere in Time*, with Eddie, this time still in 'cyborg mode with lobotomy', but now reduced to a mere head and torso, with dangling spine and holding an in utero foetus connected to him by an umbilical cord. Nice. Or not, as many people wasted no time in expressing. There is also an apple complete with yin/yang symbol within Eddie's torso, representing the good and evil of Eden and, to cap it all off, his head is on fire (an idea Riggs admitted he stole from Arthur Brown) representing inspiration. One can see that by now Eddie could be excused for being a bit fed up.

This marked the end of the development of Eddie on the covers, as by the next album he would have lost the cyborg parts and the lobotomy and have the rest of his body back. To be fair, there wasn't much further to go after this, or he would have ended up as an eyeball or an ear somewhere on the cover. In Riggs' defence, he claims the only brief he had for this cover was that it has to be 'a bit surreal', relating to prophecy and good versus evil, and that it had to be quick. He has said that he thought 'I don't really feel like painting all of Eddie this time, so I think I'll chop him off and make it a bit unpleasant'. Mission accomplished, sir!

The painting wraps around to the back, but once again it was denied a gatefold. The rear cover depicts a polar landscape with the previous Eddies encased in ice. The suggestion for the Icy Eddies came from the band, but Riggs and Dickinson have both claimed that the inspiration for the use of the frozen landscape came from them, with Dickinson remembering showing Riggs a Gustav Dore painting of a similar theme, but Riggs believing it more probably came from a documentary he watched about the North Pole. One of the few good things about the CD era in terms of artwork was that the trade-off for the smaller format helped albums like this which, in the vinyl era, would have suffered from non-gatefold sleeves. On CD, the artwork could easily be printed across the front and back cover of the CD booklet, and seen as they were intended to be seen, without the need to remove the glue and open up the album cover.

The original vinyl did come with a printed inner sleeve (clairvoyant on one side, lyrics on the other), with one particular item of interest: each song title was accompanied by a particular symbol, without explanation – a theme which has carried forward throughout future CD releases of the album. I will deal with these in the individual song entries.

'Moonchild' (Smith, Dickinson)

This opening song, with lyrics by Dickinson, sets the scene in a way as the expectant mother of the Seventh Son prepares to give birth. Lucifer is very interested in the boy, while his counterpart in Heaven, the Archangel Gabriel, is sleeping. The song is inspired in part by the Aleister Crowley novel of the same name and is filled with references to his ritual, the Liber Samekh, employed in the search for knowledge and enlightenment. Babalon, or the Whore of Babylon, represents the personification of everything attained through gratification or lust, while the mandrake's scream refers to the mandrake root, a plant which was said to scream when pulled from the ground, causing deafness or even death. In Medieval times, when it was routinely prescribed for use in pregnancy (though it has since been proven to be dangerous to pregnant women), people were advised to put wax in their ears before preparing it, for protection. Essentially, the song has Lucifer trying to goad the mother to kill her seventh son, as he fears what a child with that power could do to him.

Musically, it's a decent enough opener but never becomes as interesting as its rather progressive first 90 seconds hints at. Rather, it turns into another Maiden fast gallop, with a less than overwhelming chorus. There are decent solos by Smith (first up this time) and then, particularly, Murray, while the enthusiastic Dickinson sounds uncannily like Ian Gillan throughout the song.

The symbol accompanying the track is the Ouroborus, or the snake eating itself. It represents the endless Circle of Life – or the Wheel of Karma if you prefer. In the TV show *The X Files*, Dana Scully has a tattoo of this symbol tattooed on her lower back.

'Infinite Dreams' (Harris)

This is a much better song than 'Moonchild', both musically and lyrically. The song begins in a stately, very 'proggy' fashion, with some beautifully Hendrix-like guitar fills through some grandiose and anthemic verses until it arrives at the chorus when, by the time the 'gallop' arrives. The effect is such a contrast to its musical surroundings, that it has far greater punch and impression than 'Moonchild'. A lengthy and stunning instrumental passage goes through several time changes, but keeps on the fast, heavy yet somehow still quite catchy track throughout, with a short guitar solo from Smith being followed by an absolute cracker from Murray.

Lyrically, it deals with someone (probably the original 'seventh son', the father of the child at the centre of the narrative). He is having visions which he cannot interpret, and this gives the clue that he is not as powerful as his son (the 'seventh of the seventh'), though clearly endowed with some powers in order to be having the visions to begin with. The visions are clearly suggested as being induced by the imminent great power to be unleashed when his son is born.

The symbol for this track is the Caduceus, a wand with two entwined serpents, which was the staff of the Greek God Hermes and is often used as a symbol of harmony or balance. The serpents normally face each other, and the staff is most often winged, but the Maiden version has the serpents facing away from each other, and there are no wings atop the staff. This is the way it is normally represented in the Kabbalah, an ancient source of wisdom derived from Jewish mysticism. The relevance of this less usual depiction to the song is unclear.

It is interesting to note that the Caduceus is very often used as a symbol for the medical profession, but this is in error, as the proper traditional medical symbol is, in fact, the fairly similar Staff of Asclepius, which has only one serpent encircling the rod, and no wings. Asclepius is, in reality, thought to have been a highly skilled Ancient Greek physician, dating from around 1200BC, but through myth, he came to be known as the Greek God of Healing, and hence his staff symbolised the medical profession the world over. No-one knows for sure how the Caduceus came to be so widely used in error, but it is thought that it may in all probability have arisen from Hermes' links with alchemy, which became almost synonymous with medicine and chemistry in the 16th Century. Many people are today unaware that these symbols are two entirely different things.

'Can I Play with Madness' (Smith, Dickinson, Harris)
The first single from the album, this reached Number Three in the UK charts, and has gone on to become one of the band's best-known songs to the public – it even featured on the dire chart compilation album *Now That's What I Call Music 12*. This was great for the band's profile, of course, but it was something of a double-edged sword; the song came to overshadow everything else on the album, when in fact it is a far more simplistic effort than most of the rest of the material, musically and lyrically. The lyric, such as it is, has the man (presumably the father of the seven sons) from 'Infinite Dreams' going to see a clairvoyant to discover the meaning of his visions, and not getting along with him too well, but beyond the chorus, there isn't much there of lyrical substance. Still, it's a good, commercial rock song and has a rousing chorus superbly sung by Dickinson, so for what it is, it's very good. It just sounds a bit too cheerful and sprightly for its surroundings, a sort of 'Whistle While You Prophesy' if you like. The solo – such as it is – is by Smith.

There was an official video for the single which was, to all intents and purposes, absolutely barking mad. It concerned a group of schoolchildren

at Tintern Abbey, sketching the ruins, when one of them is criticised by
the art teacher for including Eddie's face in the sky. The teacher angrily
grabs a magazine called 'Metal Madness' from his pocket, and as he walks
while furiously perusing it, Eddie's face does actually appear in the sky
(foreshadowing the *Brave New World* cover art). The teacher, not looking
where he is going, falls into a hole. Down there he is in tunnels, so, using the
rolled-up magazine in flames as a torch, finds his way to a television (God
knows why), covered with cobwebs with Maiden playing 'The Number of the
Beast'. He then opens a fridge (I know, I know, even God doesn't know why
that's there) and finds Eddie inside. Surprise! The most interesting thing about
this piece of hopeless old tosh is that the schoolteacher is played by ex-Monty
Python man Graham Chapman, in one of his last TV appearances before he
passed away the following year. Obsessives may notice that the film of the
band shows Adrian Smith playing left-handed, so it is probably a reversed film.
Non-obsessives won't care. They would be right, but there it is anyway. Oh, and
the cover art for the single had a spring-loaded arm punching through Eddie's
head. Subtle, guys...

The symbol this time is an easy one; it's the Moon. One would think on the
surface that maybe that would have been better with 'Moonchild', but typically
in legend and mythology, the Moon is associated with both wisdom and
madness, so it actually does fit the subject matter here.

Oh, one more thing: listen to the chorus with the idea in your mind that
Bruce is asking 'Can I play with magnets?' – you will never be able to un-hear
it...

'The Evil That Men Do' (Smith, Dickinson, Harris)

The second single released from the album, this is one that is quite hard
to shoehorn into the concept with any degree of assurance. The lyrics,
such as they are, are quite vague and evocative and open to all manner of
interpretations. The most oft-claimed meaning is that the song tells about
the 'Seventh / Seventh' being conceived, and his father possibly dying in the
process, but it's a bit of a stretch, to be honest. Still, there's certainly some nice
imagery here, and musically it is a fine example of the pure Maiden sound, also
possessed of a great chorus and chart appeal without any real compromise.
This isn't 'Since You Been Gone' or 'Owner of a Lonely Heart', that's for sure.
In many ways, it's a better single than 'Can I Play with Madness', and indeed
it almost matched that song's chart success, making Number Five in the UK.
There is an official video for the single, shot on the early part of the Seventh
Tour of a Seventh Tour on 12 June 1988, in Inglewood, California. The cover
art for the single has a striking if surreal illustration of Eddie formed of smoke
and flames, with a demon atop his head holding out a contract.

The symbol for this song is a pelican, stabbing its own chest with its beak.
This refers to a myth wherein the male pelican revives its dead offspring by
tearing open its own heart and spilling its lifeblood upon them. Given the

image, it could be said that there is an argument in favour of the 'father dying in the act of conception' theory.

'Seventh Son of a Seventh Son' (Harris)

Opening the original vinyl Side Two, this is where the concept of the album really begins in earnest, with the song's lyrics directly telling of the birth of the child, and the powers he will have. Musically, it is multi-faceted throughout its almost ten-minute length: the verses are delivered to an excellent mid-paced chord sequence, while the guitars provide a superb little 'filler' riff over the top. The chorus may actually be the weakest part of the track, but that is splitting hairs somewhat. The 'song' part itself is over by around the four-minute mark in any case, with a quiet, reflective section, teased along by Nicko's nice hi-hat work. It is at this point where the sound gradually builds in intensity until a short spoken word section ushers in a heavy coda at around seven minutes. Nicko pounds away, with a great performance, while Murray takes two solos and then Smith two more. It's a piece which shows off the new Maiden progressive influence really well.

The symbol this time may look like a simple Sun, but In fact it represents the planet Venus, symbolising the supervision of new life and rebirth, which does fit the 'theme' well enough.

'The Prophecy' (Murray, Harris)

In which our hero attempts to use his powers for good, but with predictably unsuccessful results. He has a vision of a disaster befalling a village and warns them to leave in time. Of course, they don't believe him and stay put. The unspecified disaster happens, and they now all proceed to 'blame the messenger', accusing him of having put a curse on the village. There's a real sense straight away that this guy simply can't win.

The reference to hearing 'the cry of the seven whistlers' comes from an old belief in UK folklore of seven birds, or spirits, who can be heard to call out before a disaster of some kind. These are mentioned in the poetry of Wordsworth and, further back, in Spenser's *Faerie Queen*. This myth led to a belief among such hazardous occupations as mining and sailing that whistling itself was unlucky. Indeed, there are records going back to Victorian England, referring to whole groups of coal miners refusing to go underground after hearing this sinister sound. It has been suggested that the distinctive cry of the curlew is at the heart of the belief.

Musically, this is another home run, being another chugging, nicely paced song with a nice, slow introduction and a very unusual Maiden outro consisting of a minute or so of beautifully delicate acoustic guitar. This latter section may be what got Dave Murray his writing credit. The symbol for this one is a common one, once again, among the ancient Egyptians, but also the Sumerians, Assyrians, Babylonians and other ancient cultures: the Winged Disc. The disc in question may be an eye (it was often known as the Eye of Horus by the Egyptians) or the Sun. In India, it was known as the Eye of Shiva, which is to say, Satan. The connection here may be that Lucifer has created the disaster in the hope of the 'Seventh / Seventh' turning against his ungrateful fellow men and following him.

'The Clairvoyant' (Harris)
Things don't go well for our all-seeing hero here, as his visions become more and more vivid, and he ultimately perishes – presumably taking his own life. In truth, this is a relatively slight song and not one of the strongest on the album. Even the guitar solo, by Murray, seems a little bit 'by numbers'. It's a reasonable example of the Maiden sound at that time, but without anything to make it stand out, beyond advancing the plot. Nice bass intro from Harris, mind you. A live version of this was released as a single, with live versions of 'The Prisoner' and (12" only) 'Heaven Can Wait' on the flip. It made Number Six on the UK singles chart, so what do I know? Interestingly, Steve Harris has said that he got the initial idea for this song from hearing a news report of the death of noted psychic Doris Stokes, and wondering whether she was able to foretell her own demise.

The symbol is an odd one; a chalice with three snakes coming out of it. There is a definite inspiration behind this one though, being that of St. John, writer of the fourth Gospel and the *Book of Revelations*. He was supposedly given a cup of poisoned wine to drink on one occasion, but he blessed it before drinking, and the poison departed in the form of three serpents.

'Only the Good Die Young' (Harris, Dickinson)
In which the ill-fated Seventh Son sides with Lucifer and delivers his final kiss-off to humanity. There are pot-shots at Christianity here ('your bishops and guilt'), and also those villagers who preferred to believe in a man walking on water than his very real warnings. One can understand his bitterness, really. Musically it is a strange one – it's a very strong way to close the album, with a deliciously sardonic delivery from Bruce and a strong chorus, but it is far too short. After around four minutes it just seems to be getting going and building into a lengthy instrumental tour de force to finish the album on, when it suddenly just stops. A reprise of the four lines which opened the first track provides a nice bookend, but it's all a little anticlimactic – especially seeing as, at under 44 minutes, it's a shorter album than either of the last two. Still, a good album overall, for sure, if not quite as adventurous as it could have been. Bruce was right on the money about the concept not going far enough, and there's a definite sense musically that the band, particularly Harris and Dickinson, really wanted to stretch out and experiment but were afraid to go too far. Smith plays the first solo and Murray the second, incidentally – while in between them, Harris gets in on the action with a short bass solo.

The final symbol here is a hand holding a downward pointing arrow with a crossbar and a triangle atop it, with what looks like flames on the top of the whole thing. This is actually the alchemical symbol for sulphur, so the connection with taking the devil's side and damnation is a clear one.

Related songs:
'Black Bart Blues' (Harris, Dickinson)
There is a story behind this fairly throwaway B-side (from the 'Can I Play with Madness' single). 'Black Bart' was, in fact, a suit of armour that Bruce Dickinson bought from an out-of-the-way gas station in the US – because they all sell them, right? Just next to the rack of magazines. Anyhow, for whatever reason, there were three of these lined up outside. It was far from a working, wearable suit, as it was all welded together for a start, but that tacky 'kitsch' nature attracted him even more, and so Bart was duly bought and installed in the back lounge of the tour bus. That's the area where all of the (Bruce's words) 'nefarious shagging' went on. So, the main thrust of the song emphasises that there isn't much to which Bart hasn't been a witness.

Musically it's a straight-ahead rocker without a whole lot to particularly recommend it, but there is an infectious sense of fun about it, and also a hint of a Frank Zappa influence in the snippets of dialogue between Dickinson and the 'groupie', and also in some of the little asides in the lyrics. The song finishes with a lengthy series of snippets of, mainly, Nicko being, well, Nicko, including a few of his Idi Amin impressions. You won't give it repeated listens...

'Massacre' (Lynott, Gorham, Downey)
A cover of Thin Lizzy's song from their 1976 album *Johnny the Fox*, it's easy to see why Maiden wanted to have a crack at this, as it concerns the same subject matter as 'The Trooper' – that is to say the Charge of the Light Brigade in the Crimean War – and, of course, Lizzy were one of the pioneers of the twin lead guitar sound that Maiden embraced from Day One. They do it well, but it's put together in such a straightforward way that it can't be said to improve on the original. It's a good effort, though. Adrian Smith takes the solo.

The other single from the album, 'The Clairvoyant', was backed with newly recorded studio versions of 'Prowler' and 'Charlotte the Harlot' from the debut album. There isn't a whole lot to say about them, really. Bruce sings them, and the production is better. There, I said it.

No Prayer for the Dying

Personnel:
Bruce Dickinson: vocals
Dave Murray: guitars,
Janick Gers: guitars
Steve Harris: bass guitar
Nicko McBrain: drums
With:
Michael Kenney: keyboards
Record Label: EMI (UK), Epic (US)
Recorded: June-Sept 1990, produced by Martin Birch
Release date: 1 October 1990
Highest chart places: UK: 2, USA: 17
Running time: 43:42

In the first Maiden line-up change since Clive Burr's departure following *The Number of the Beast* – and a significant one at that – Adrian Smith left the band during preparations for this album, stating his unhappiness with the direction the album was taking, and he only contributed writing on one song.

His replacement was Janick Gers, from Hartlepool. Born in 1957, he had begun his musical career in the North East band White Spirit. They were lumped in with the NWOBHM, but in fact were more akin to Deep Purple and other more progressive bands, with their extensive use of keyboards and predilection for lengthy epics. They regularly closed their live shows with an astonishing version of 'Child in Time' and were even known to tackle Pink Floyd's 'Shine On You Crazy Diamond' on occasion. Having seen the band live on several occasions, I can personally attest to how good they were, and Gers was always the man who stood out. After the band were publicly acclaimed by Ian Gillan on the radio and (along with Quartz) invited to support his band, Gillan, on the *Glory Road* UK tour, White Spirit split and Gers took up the invitation to join Gillan as replacement for the departing Bernie Tormé. Gillan themselves split when Ian took the chance to hook up again with the reunited Deep Purple in 1984, and Gers took a degree in Humanities as well as briefly joining Paul Di'Anno and Clive Burr in a project titled Gogmagog. After playing on ex-Marillion vocalist Fish's debut album *Vigil in a Wilderness of Mirrors*, he collaborated with Bruce Dickinson on the latter's first solo album *Tattooed Millionaire*, released in May 1990. The pair co-wrote almost all of the material, with Gers supplying all of the guitars, so the invitation to join Maiden was a natural one.

After the more progressive approach, and synthesizer use, of the previous two albums, Steve Harris had said that he wanted this one to have a more stripped back, 'street-level' sound. Smith said that he felt this was a step backwards, and after he left, he started a family and did not play on stage again for two years. With Gers stepping in during the recording, the guitarist did not arrive in time to contribute to any of the writing.

In line with this freshly stripped-down approach (it is the only Maiden album without a song breaking the six-minute barrier), the band forsook the expensive studios and undertook the recording in a barn on Harris's property, a move looked back on later by Dickinson as being disastrous to the band's sound, although he admitted that he had been as complicit as anyone in the decision.

Album Cover:

Another Riggs cover here, but one with an interesting history. The cover as originally released features Eddie (now restored to a full body and un-lobotomised brain) bursting out of a grave (seen from above) and grabbing a hapless gravedigger by the neck. The gravedigger was made to strongly resemble manager Rod Smallwood, who hated the figure so much that he insisted that the 1998 reissue CD had it removed from the picture so that Eddie now just reaches toward the viewer. In another change, an inscription was added to a plaque on the front cover. It was left blank on the original by Riggs in order for the band to add their own words, which for some reason they never did. On the reissue it now read 'After the Daylight, The Night of Pain, That is not Dead, Which Can Rise Again', which was nice and cheerful. The rear cover of the original album was pure tedium, with a photo of the band, all arms-around-shoulders and 'team-bonding' under the stark band names and tracklisting. A long way from *Somewhere in Time* and *Powerslave*, that's for sure. The reissued CD has them standing in a graveyard, and isn't much better. There was an inner sleeve with the vinyl, having lyrics on a background of Eddie on one side and a band photo on the other. It wasn't too exciting.

'Tailgunner' (Harris, Dickinson)

'Surely we've been here before' is an immediate reaction on being confronted with this WWII flying opus, very similar to the earlier– and better – 'Aces High'.Not that it's a bad song – indeed, the insidious introductory riff which continues beneath the verses, complete with slashing power chords, sneaks its way into your brain and makes its home there. The chorus, however, is jarring and destroys that carefully built up atmosphere at a stroke. The lyrics, too, are fairly banal. They have been interpreted by some as a subtly sardonic anti-war comment and by others at face value as a triumphalist war cry. Whatever the intent, lines like 'Cologne and Frankfurt – have some more!' sound heavy-handed in the extreme. Gers takes the first solo here with 20 seconds to make his first impression – it's not his best or most fluid. Murray takes over with little greater success. Overall, the song is okay. It's not bad, it's not great. It's okay. But was that good enough for Iron Maiden?

The lyrics make some historical observations: the carpet-bombing of Dresden in 1945 (tactically unnecessary) is alluded to, as are of course the bombings of Cologne and Frankfurt, and the Enola Gay mentioned in the second verse was the plane carrying the atomic bomb dropped on Hiroshima. Flown by pilot

Paul Tibbets, the name comes from a mix of his mother's name(Gay) and an inversion of the word 'alone'. 'Tail-end Charlie' was an actual nickname given to tail gunners in WWII, and comes from Charles Cooper, the first commissioned tail gunner in the RAF in WWII. The line 'Nail that Fokker, kill that son' is clumsy and obvious in its use of the word 'Fokker' instead of the profanity implied – in fact, the German forces used no Fokkers at all during the conflict, something which both Harris and Dickinson would surely know.

Dickinson has said that the name came from a porn film, with the title 'Tailgunner' being an obvious reference to the target area in question. He has said that he penned the wartime lyrics as he was unable to write about being a 'tail gunner' in the other sense. We should be thankful...

'Holy Smoke' (Harris, Dickinson)

The first single from the album (the single actually came first by a few weeks) saw Maiden taking on the theme of hypocritical TV evangelists in a clever and witty lyric. There are references to a few real-life US 'televangelists' (Jimmy Swaggart being immortalised as Jimmy Reptile), and the whole thing is delivered in an upbeat, cheery fashion which seems to fit the lyric to perfection. The single reached Number Three in the UK charts, and it is easy to see why as the song boasts an instantly memorable chorus hook.

The official video for the single also could only have helped, as it is enormous fun to watch, with the band making no attempt to take themselves remotely seriously. Shot on Harris's farm, and featuring some shots of the band rehearsing in his soon-to-be-named Barnyard Studios location (in his barn, surprisingly enough), the video contains shots of Dickinson cavorting in a field of flowers wearing a bright pink shirt as he sings. Harris rides on a tractor driven by long-term Maiden friend and roadie Vic Vella, and Murray and Gers shred away in a river and a swimming pool respectively. Martin Birch appears as a long-haired, leather-clad oaf surrounded by a bevy of beauties (displaying some distressingly assless leather pants at one point). Harris's faithful bass tech Michael Kenney is also briefly glimpsed working on his bass. The overall feel is the knockabout kind of looning around that the Beatles introduced in *Help!* and the Monkees went on to run with, and it's all great fun. The single sleeve featured a Riggs illustration of Eddie standing atop a bonfire, burning TVs with these preachers on them.

'No Prayer for the Dying' (Harris)

This is a very different type of song, with the title track coming in on a restrained, laid-back opening with a bed of stirringly melodic guitar lines. The lyric, delivered in quite a heartfelt manner by Bruce, sees the protagonist asking God for meaning in his troubled life. It's hard to see the connection to the title since he is clearly not about to die. After the two-minute mark, things get kicked up a notch tempo-wise, and Murray (twice) and Gers (in the middle) get to trade solos. It all breaks down again at the end and finishes on the same stirring note as it began. An excellent song, it would have perhaps been better a little longer, to stretch out a little

'Public Enema Number One' (Murray, Dickinson)
This song actually has a serious message, though the hopelessly puerile pun in the title doesn't do it any favours. As Dickinson has explained, it's about the environment, and specifically what he calls 'green hypocrites' who talk about environmental issues while contributing to the problem by their actions. There are some nice turns of phrase in the lyric ('When the lights go greed' when talking about the guy in his fast car escaping the city, for example), but you just look at that title and think 'come on guys, you're better than that'.

Musically, this is pretty nondescript. The verses have a decent bite to them, but the chorus is weak, despite a bit of a kick coming in the second chorus line. Someone, who I believe to be Nicko (it usually is!) kicks the song off with a laugh and ends it with what sounds like a distant cry of 'Wankers!' – that doesn't really aid and abet a serious political message either if we're honest. Murray does the solo here, but few people care all that much in all probability. A low point on an album generally rated among Maiden's worst.

'Fates Warning' (Murray, Harris)
A good song here, although at the same time one which illustrates the problems this album has in a nutshell. The lyric is quite nice, a rumination on the fact that everyone's life hangs by a thread, to be saved or lost on a simple twist of fate – even if it seems clear that there should be an apostrophe in the word 'Fate's'! Musically things are also nice. A beautiful laid back intro with some lyrically melodic guitar work makes you partly sorry when it is swept away by a chugging riff nearly a minute in. Said riff powers the verses, and is very good, and there is some nice twin lead playing in the instrumental section, in between solos from Dave and then Janick.

Those are the good points. Unfortunately, all of those nice musical ideas are shoehorned into just over four minutes, when the intro should have been used further or at least returned to, and it's simply too short. Just an album or two previously this sort of composition would have been allowed to 'breathe' over a six or seven-minute length, but here it's stifled as if the band just want to get it done and out of the way. Sure, Harris wanted to strip things back a bit, but even on the first album they had 'Remember Tomorrow' and 'Phantom of the Opera'. Also, Bruce's vocals are, as on many tracks on this album, much too harsh and sound forced as well. The great operatic release of 'Run to the Hills' or 'Ancient Mariner' is barely in evidence, which is rather a shame. In this case, it's 'nice song, wish I could sing it better, but I'm too "street" now, you see'. On their classic albums, Maiden were such a great band they could make the weakest material sound at least good – at this point they manage to make the greatest material sound merely good, which is a shame.

This one has never been played live, which is very strange.

'The Assassin' (Harris)

Oh dear. If the previous track was an example of a good song not being given enough justice, this one is simply a bit of a barrel-scraping exercise, both musically and lyrically. There is a gradual build-up at the beginning, which leads you to expect that it will burst into life at some point, but it just somehow never does. By the end of the first verse that much has become evident.

Bruce's vocals are dreadful here by his own stratospheric standards. He tries to impart some sense of 'film noir' grittiness but just ends up half-growling and half-singing. That is just describing the verses, however – the chorus is a different matter entirely. It's worse. Anyone thinking the backing vocals in the chorus of 'Die With Your Boots On' were a low point, may revise their opinion here, as Bruce's vain attempt to make 'Better watch out, 'cos I'm the assassin' try to sound menacing is met with what sounds like a couple of extras from *West Side Story* popping their heads around the door, clicking their fingers and intoning 'Better watch out! Better watch out!'

It's grim stuff, to be honest. Right from the first line, with 'Now the contract's out, they've put the word about', just thinking about the drop off from 'Revelations' or 'Ancient Mariner' to this is enough to make one's head hurt. It's almost as if they'd just noticed how Judas Priest had spent a decade dumbing down their approach and thought 'we can do that!' – well yeah, you can guys. But you never, ever should. Murray contributes the opening run of the mill solo while Janick takes that baton and runs with it. Well, the record can only go up now...

'Run Silent, Run Deep' (Harris, Dickinson)

And hallelujah, improve it does right away with this submarine-themed wartime song with a Dickinson lyric based on the 1958 film of the same name, starring Clark Gable and Burt Lancaster. In fact, the lyric is from one of his rejected songs for *Somewhere in Time*, which he suggested to Harris for a song he had that lacked words. Once again, there is a great atmospheric opening, all churning watery background and suchlike, but on this occasion when the band crash in with a marching brute-rocker it actually works. The very first line 'The convoy lights are dead ahead' puts the listener into the action, front and centre. Even the chorus has Bruce doing an old-fashioned soaring vocal again, as if to prove he still can when he wants to!

It's not all great news – the solos by Gers and then Murray are fairly weak and prevent the song from having the real classic instrumental section which would make it a real winner, but it's an undeniably good effort. Still too short though, at four-and-a-half minutes. They just didn't seem to want to develop the songs on this album for some reason.

'Hooks in You' (Dickinson, Smith)

Hang on, this is an AC/DC track surely ... (checks label) ... oh no, it is still Iron Maiden. I can't have been the only one to have had this sort of reaction when first hearing this song, surely? From the opening line 'I got the keys to view at number 22', Bruce delivers this as pure Brian Johnson, and within those parameters, it's quite entertaining. But there is no way in this world that this should ever have been an Iron Maiden song by every definition of their career so far. Mind you, apart from the AC/DC riffery and Bruce's best Johnson-isms, there is a nice instrumental section with Janick starting the solo before Murray joins in and they finish it together.

Dickinson has explained that the idea for the lyric came from the time he went to look at a house with his wife, with a view to buying it. It was owned, he says, 'by three gay guys', of whom 'one was obviously into S&M and leather and stuff, and in one room there were these enormous industrial hooks screwed into the ceiling'. He says his mind 'boggled' at what these could have been used for, and wrote the song from the viewpoint of finding a 'Mr and Mrs Average' with these hooks. He claims that the final verse, with its reference to concrete, refers to the man believing his wife has been unfaithful and setting her in concrete in the foundations. Which seems a little extreme, to be honest. Oh, and no – they didn't buy the house!

Many people view this as another song in the 'Charlotte' series, because of the address being Number 22, but nothing else seems to fit the idea, so it is possibly equally likely that 22 was simply there to rhyme with 'keys to view'.

'Bring Your Daughter... to the Slaughter' (Dickinson)
This song, when released as a single, made Number One in the UK charts, the only Iron Maiden song to do so. I should probably pause to let that sink in because it's a quite shocking fact. Without doubt one of the most dumbed-down, lowest common denominator tracks the band ever released, to see it reach that level of popularity was shocking, and in many ways, it really didn't do the band any favours at that time.

To put things into historical context, this was originally a Bruce Dickinson song. He was recording his first solo album, *Tattooed Millionaire*, and was asked to do a song for the soundtrack of the film *A Nightmare on Elm Street 5: The Dream Child*. This was the latest instalment in a film series which had already passed its expiration date some years earlier, so there clearly wasn't a need for anything highbrow. Collaborating with Janick Gers, Bruce's version of the song is actually better than Maiden's – it's taken at a slightly slower pace, has some excellent double-tracked vocals in the chorus (which needs all the help it can get!), and it has more atmosphere in general. Steve Harris heard something he thought was right for Maiden, and persuaded Bruce to leave it off his solo album. The Maiden arrangement promptly took the song at a breakneck pace, rendering it even more cheesy and producing the kind of schlock-horror which was everything 'The Number of the Beast' was not.

The single cover art contains one interesting detail of note: the door behind Eddie and the mysterious woman in red (supposedly inspired by Jessica Rabbit from the film *Who Framed Roger Rabbit?*) reads 'The Paradise Club'. This was the title of a little-remembered UK TV show of that name which ran from '89 to '90, and in one episode of which Dickinson actually starred, along with his band, who made an appearance playing as a band named 'Fraud Squad'!

There was an official video clip, which intercut live footage with clips from an old 1960 horror film called *City of the Dead* (*Horror Hotel* in the US). Perhaps this was in the hope that people would be convinced that the song was intended to evoke creepy old black and white suspense and fear. In the event, most people couldn't care less about the lyrics, while those that did listen would be left in no doubt as to the clumsily executed sexual innuendo which strays into some questionable areas. The song has not been played live for almost two decades now, which would appear to speak volumes about something so successful. Let's draw a veil over it, and move on to...

'Mother Russia' (Harris)

A much more ambitious song to finish the album on – and the first one to run to over five minutes! Tackling the subject of the reforms going on in Russia at the time, through Mikhail Gorbachev's 'Glasnost' initiative, it is at least trying to tackle something a little more mature and weightier than the last couple of efforts. Unfortunately, it really doesn't do it all that well.

Lyrically, things are far too simplistic to make any point of note, and the old Harris habit of putting in hopelessly uneven numbers of syllables returns with a vengeance. Poor old Bruce struggles manfully to make 'dance of the Tsars' have the same musical scansion as 'be proud of what you are'. It's almost as if Harris thought 'come on, let's have something for the literate old guard to close the album', without really having any actual inspiration. The song is often credited with being a sarcastic and mocking attack on Russia's perceived reforms at the time, but to be honest, there isn't really enough here to make a decision either way on that point.

Musically, the track has its moments, but it is clumsy and sounds bolted together. At around the two-minute mark, there is a section where things get properly epic sounding for a while (thanks to some strategically deployed synths), and the solo section where Murray and Gers trade solos five times is quite exhilarating. The main riff, however, is clunky and leaden-footed, with even the irrepressible Nicko sounding as if he is hitting things with heavy broom handles, and Bruce has a thankless task to raise the sound of the verses.

Ultimately, it's too little too late to save a record which, while it may not be a bad album exactly, is certainly a bad Iron Maiden album. It's stripped back and dumbed down too far, with the whole point of the early Maiden sound missed completely – back then it was punky sounding, energetic music which strove to be something more. This album is dull-sounding, simplistic rock which strives to be nothing more. And that's a shame.

Related songs:

'All in Your Mind' (Bromham)

The B-side to 'Holy Smoke', this is a cover of a song by UK band Stray, from their 1970 debut album. Long-time favourites of Harris, Stray (led by frontman Del Bromham) were the quintessential 'journeyman' band in the UK in the 1970s. For years, it seemed, you could hardly see a festival bill without Stray propping up one of the days. An excellent band, they somehow never made fanatically attended small gigs and a series of good albums translate into wider success. Maiden's version of this one simplifies the nine-minute original to half that length, stripping out the instrumental excesses and delivering a lean and mean rendition. Bruce's voice is reduced to a snarling sort of growl, but that is to keep to the spirit of the original. Gers takes all of the solos here. A nice effort.

'Kill Me (Ce Soir)' (Kooymans, Hay, Fenton)
The third track on the 'Holy Smoke' 12-inch single, this is another cover, this time of a song by the Dutch band Golden Earring, who had released their landmark album *Moontan* in 1973. They followed this up with *Switch*, a disappointing release overall, but redeemed by this one enduring classic, telling the story of a rock star gunned down following the release of an outspoken and controversially political record. This version is much more aggressive, while the original is more sinister and 'proggy', but it's nonetheless a decent attempt at something which seems outside of the band's comfort zone. There is too much of the growling vocal from Bruce this time, though.

'I'm A Mover' (Fraser, Rodgers)
The B-side to 'Bring Your Daughter... to the Slaughter', this Free classic is a baffling selection to cover. Free were well known for having a swagger to their bluesy rock, being the masters of leaving space between the notes for the song to breathe. Iron Maiden, by the same token, would be more likely to approach a space between notes with a cry of 'A space! Quickly, kill it with a guitar solo!' Different times, different bands. In fact, after a leaden-footed start, in which the song is stifled rather than being allowed to breathe by the dead production sound and a band who were not really big on 'swing' or indeed 'soul', they grow into it. The solos are nice, and by the end they've started to get inside the song a bit more. It's a brave effort.

'Communication Breakdown' (Page, Jones, Bonham)
We are on safer ground here, as the guys blast through this track from Led Zeppelin's debut album for the '...Daughter...' 12-inch as if they are having an absolute ball. Right in their wheelhouse, it's a good, if inessential, version, with Bruce channelling his inner Plant for all he's worth!

Fear of the Dark
Personnel:
Bruce Dickinson: vocals
Dave Murray: guitars
Janick Gers: guitars
Steve Harris: bass guitar
Nicko McBrain: drums
With:
Michael Kenney - keyboards
Record Label: EMI (UK), Epic (US)
Recorded: Jan-April 1992, produced by Martin Birch and Steve Harris
Release date: 11 May 1992.
Highest chart places: UK: 1, USA: 12
Running time: 57:58

After the disappointing sonic results from the recording of *No Prayer for the Dying* in Steve Harris' barn, he had it completely refitted with a professional studio set-up (naming it Barnyard Studios), and the band reconvened there to record this album in early 1992. The results were mixed, with Dickinson's vocals coming in for a lot of criticism. At almost an hour long, it was the first double vinyl studio album the band had released, though in fairness it could easily have been trimmed down by three tracks or so and left as a single disc without sacrificing any quality.

This would prove to be the last Maiden album with Bruce at the mic for seven years, as he left after the tour to pursue a solo career, which in fact, led to a string of excellent albums under his own name. It would also be the last album worked on by Martin Birch, who retired after its release. Steve Harris co-produced this one with Birch, so it is safe to assume that there was an amount of 'knowledge transfer' going on within their working relationship.

Album Cover:
It was all change in the artwork department as well, with this being the first Maiden cover not to be done by Derek Riggs. In fact, Riggs did submit a design, but the band preferred the one done by Melvyn Grant, a popular illustrator of science fiction and fantasy novels. The Grant design is indeed effective, depicting Eddie as – in the words of Maiden biographer Mick Wall – 'some sort of Nosferatu tree figure leering at the moon'. If you look closely, he appears to be part of the tree itself, and there seems to be another creature of some sort right behind him. The use of blue and black in the design is very atmospheric and effective, but sadly Riggs' submission does not seem to be available to compare and contrast. Certainly, the band's stated aim was to give Eddie an overhaul, making him less cartoony and more sinister, and in this case that was achieved.

The cover was of necessity a gatefold, with the double vinyl, but this was at the barrel-end of the original vinyl culture, and sales were going over more to

CD every year. The rear cover has the tracklisting along with the band standing in front of some sort of monstrous flying creature, while the inner gatefold spread has the lyrics along with band photos and credits.

'Be Quick or Be Dead' (Dickinson, Gers)

The first single from the album, this is a very fast-paced number which seems to take some influence from the Thrash Metal movement. There is energy in spades, and the main riff is a marvellously propulsive one, storming along like an uncontrollable runaway train threatening to leave the tracks at any moment. It made Number Two in the UK singles chart, which is hard to believe now given the way it has been largely forgotten as a single release. What spoils things a little is Dickinson's strangled vocal, which leaves us several bus journeys back from where we found him a few short years before this. Happily, he would rediscover his clarity and range and relocate his missing high notes in the years to come.

Lyrically, Bruce leads us into a world of political intrigue, where shadowy CEOs bleed their employees dry in a world where one must, in order to survive, be 'quick or dead'. It's a little like 'Holy Smoke' on the previous album, but not as successful as there is less in terms of verse content and more of the repeated chorus.The solos are by Gers first and Murray second, and are both excellent. Derek Riggs returned for the single sleeve design, but it is a weak cartoon sort of effort and looks like a kind of 'Eddie on Wall Street', which fails to work on any level.

'From Here to Eternity' (Harris)

Ah, it's a Steve Harris song, and it's called 'From Here to Eternity' – this will be based on the film of that name, right? Wrong. Very wrong, as it happens. Despite its evocative title, this is actually another song in that pesky 'Charlotte the Harlot' series, in which Charlotte has now graduated to going on a motorcycle ride with what may be the devil or may simply be a random biker. One look at the lyric is enough to evoke nostalgic memories of 'Ancient Mariner' or 'Loneliness of the Long Distance Runner' with a heavy sigh. The first two lines read 'She fell in love with his greasy machine / She leaned over and licked his kickstart clean'. Nope, we're not going to learn about Alexander the Great and his tactical acuity on this occasion, guys. Still, killing Charlotte off in a crash (spoiler alert!) in this one did mean that future entries in this series would be unlikely.

The official video for the single has the band playing among ruins in a sort of *Mad Max*-style landscape, atop a giant rock pillar, intercut with odd scenes, including a biker wedding. The chorus is fairly catchy in a shouty, AC/DC way, and the solos (Murray then Gers) are superb, but taken as a whole the song is crass, written-to-be-a-single, sub-*Beavis and Butthead* nonsense. At least it only made Number 21 on the singles chart. Not a strong start to the album, but things were about to get better...

'Afraid to Shoot Strangers' (Harris)

With song number three, things get a whole lot more serious, both musically and lyrically. Let's take the lyrics first, as they have been the cause of some controversy ever since the album's release. The song takes the perspective of a soldier in the Gulf War, looking inside his mind before the fighting. He isn't afraid to fight or die, he says, but it is implicit that what keeps him awake is the thought of having to kill 'strangers', and trying to justify the cause to himself. So far so good, and indeed powerful, but it is at this point that people start to disagree. While many laud this as an anti-war song of some importance, others look at it as a song that condones the reasons behind the conflict, for which 'divisive' doesn't even cover it. Bruce has said, before a major show at Donington, that it is about men having to fight who don't even want to be there. However, those attacking Harris for his supposed political views have responded to this by claiming that Bruce either didn't grasp what he was getting at, or else was justifying the song to himself in order to be able to sing it.

To my mind, this is all meaningless discussion. Much of the greatest music in the world has been written by people with whom some of the more fervent listeners would vehemently disagree, regarding their view of the world. At the end of the day, it is a few lines in the song. The offending lines, about having to end a corrupt regime, while arguably not the prime reason for the conflict, should be looked on either as one man's opinion or, let us not forget, quite possibly just what the soldier in the song is telling himself in order to go through with the song's events.

Such arguments, while interesting enough in themselves, can get in the way of appreciating what matters, which is the music, and it's very good on this occasion. The song starts with a lengthy slow, atmospheric intro, with the sound gradually filling out as Dickinson sings the verses (which all come before the repeated chorus line). And he delivers it well. When the full band come in after just over two-and-a-half minutes, it is not with a big Maiden galloping riff as one would perhaps expect, but instead an instrumental section quite reminiscent of Wishbone Ash and their landmark album *Argus*. At the four-minute mark, a huge piledriving riff comes in and Janick takes the first solo with great aplomb. This is nothing, however, compared to Murray's absolutely masterful solo after the repetitive chorus mantra of the song title. Toward the end, that Wishbone Ash bit comes in again – this time very close in sound to the Wishbone track 'Throw Down the Sword', and the song dies away into a peaceful end. It's a great track and really gets the album going. It is good to see them stretching out to almost seven minutes, as well.

'Fear is the Key' (Dickinson, Gers)

Another 'serious message' song here, as the attention of the band, turns to the AIDS epidemic and widespread fear during the '80s and '90s. Indeed, the catalyst for the song was the death of Freddie Mercury which occurred during the writing of the album, leading to the line 'nobody cares until somebody famous dies'. The twin beams of the song are turned on the nostalgic past of sexual freedom and permissiveness and also the present-day climate of fear and misinformation, which Bruce appears to be claiming is being spread to keep people in check. An arguable point, but again, opinions in a song. They're all valid. The more concerning thing is the creeping doubt as to whether there is a sense of 'cause of the day' creeping into the band's writing, after the likes of 'Holy Smoke' and 'Be Quick or Be Dead' on the last album. Up until this point, Maiden had never been a political band, taking up the cudgels about current affairs, and while that may be laudable, there was a slight sense of missing the old literary epics.

Musically, the song is excellent, apart from one thing. And that thing is 'Perfect Strangers' by Deep Purple, to which this track bears such a striking resemblance that it is hard to ignore (of course, one could say that the Deep Purple track was itself born of Led Zeppelin's 'Kashmir', but that's another matter entirely). During a semi-spoken part toward the end, Bruce even starts to sound exactly like Ian Gillan. There's a pleasingly epic quality here for sure, but it is perhaps too close to its inspiration (Gers' first band White Spirit had been accused at times of being very Purple-influenced). It's a good track, but how good depends on your opinion of the lyrics and your 'Perfect Strangers' threshold...

'Childhood's End' (Harris)

Aha, you might say on seeing this song title. The Arthur C. Clarke Science Fiction classic, Mr Harris has been reading again. Sadly, however, this is not the case, as we are looking at the state of the world again, and it's utterly hopeless as all there is worldwide is misery. Aw, c'mon Steve, watch a film already! The relatively short lyric to this contains the phrases 'no life, no hope', 'no love', 'pain and fear', the agonies of all-out war', 'suffering and pain', 'sadness and tears', 'desperation', 'contaminated waters', 'decay' and 'waiting for disease to strike'. So, not much in the way of laughs then.

There is an argument for saying that telling things like they are is the only thing to do, and that's fine in itself, but there are two flaws with that position. Firstly, as alluded to already, this sort of social commentary has never been Maiden's forte – everyone has their niche, and just as Billy Bragg wouldn't be expected to write 'Rime of the Ancient Mariner', Maiden seem equally awkward doing this. Secondly, and this refers just to this track, it is so over the top in its depressing depiction of us all going to hell in a handbasket that it ends up becoming a parody of itself. It's too extreme to be taken seriously.

Musically, it's okay without being in any way memorable, and it isn't too surprising that the band have never played it live. There are decent solos though, from Gers then Murray.

'Wasting Love' (Harris)

Or, as it might be known, Iron Leppard. No that's probably a bit harsh, but this earnest power ballad certainly has more than a whiff of big production 'hair metal' around it. The subject matter this time is the loneliness brought about by empty sexual conquests outside the context of love. Jeez, somebody really soured these guys' cornflakes at this time, didn't they? To be fair to this song, once the riffs start coming in, there is a fair bit of melodic power, while Janick solos as if his life is at stake, or at least as if he's auditioning for Whitesnake at any rate. It's an enjoyable melodic rock song, but is it Maiden? Not on my watch.

There is an official video (this was the third single from the album, though only released in the Netherlands, I believe), which is hilarious in an unintentional way. Shots of the band playing fight for space with intercut scenes which are all flickering flames, lovers in the shadows, and muscular men in white shirts with cold, empty eyes. It's like a Mills and Boon romantic bodice-ripper novel brought to life, at least until the end when an exorcising priest and someone with angel wings appear as if they have wandered in from another video. Track it down and watch it – it's so terrible that you can't look away.

'The Fugitive' (Harris)
You remember the classic TV series from the '60s? It was remade as an acceptable 1993 film with Harrison Ford and then as a completely unacceptable later TV series, which should be wiped from the Earth. Well, the good news is that Popular Culture Buff Harris is back because this actually is about the TV show. True, the lyrics don't exactly go into any sort of profound depth, but it's nice to have some traditional Maiden subject matter again.

It's pretty good musically, as well, apart from a hopeless chorus. There is a sinewy riff winding its way behind the verses which is very much driven by Harris, who is superlative on bass throughout this one. Indeed, the guitars give him the space to play in, which ticks another 'old Maiden' box. Bruce shows off his range for one of the few moments on the album, which is great to hear. Gers and then Murray pull out a couple of great solos as well, as the music gets faster and harder, with Janick taking the plaudits on this occasion, by a short head.

'Chains of Misery' (Dickinson, Murray)
Well, at least there is no heavy socio-political commentary here, as this rather slight, but enjoyable, track sees Dickinson having fun with the subject of that 'little devil' on your shoulder which, in its popular image, whispers poor advice and makes you do bad things. It's a sprightly enough rocker, with Murray doing all of the soloing, but there is somehow no more depth to the music than the lyrics. The real nadir is the football-terrace sounding nature of the backing vocalists delivering the 'Chains of misery' line. Fluff, but not bad fluff for what it is.

'The Apparition' (Harris, Gers)
In which Iron Maiden don masks and do their best Deep Purple routine – well, that's not far from the truth as this jagged clunker could have fit seamlessly

onto *In Rock* or *Fireball*. Dickinson has occasionally had a propensity to sound a little like Ian Gillan in the past, but never more than this. Even the little 'asides' at the end of each couplet are pure Gillan.

Lyrically, this is an odd one from Harris. The apparition in question is a ghost which is about to 'move on', but for some reason stays around long enough to deliver a stream of fortune cookie snippets of advice and wisdom, like some kind of disembodied Hyde Park Corner speaker. Essentially, it is 'The World According to Steve Harris', with added ectoplasm. And not only is it lyrically atypical for Maiden, musically it goes against all expectations from the moment Bruce comes straight in, with the full band, from the first second with no introduction of any kind, the first time Maiden have done this. The only part of the track which sounds reassuringly 'Maiden' is the instrumental mid-song, when the tempo kicks up a notch and Gers, Murray and then Gers again deliver three fluid and exciting solos. Straight away, however, it's back to the metronomic sledgehammer of the verses again. There's no variation whatsoever, no changes, no chorus and little emotion. Call an exorcist, this one has to go.

'Judas Be My Guide' (Dickinson, Murray)

Now *this*, this is more like it! One of Maiden's shortest ever songs, at just a shade over three minutes, this is nevertheless an overlooked classic, both lyrically and musically. The song developed from a line 'Take me to Jesus... with Judas my guide' in the song 'Under the Gun' from Bruce's solo album *Tattooed Millionaire*. He thought the phrase was worthy of its own song – and rightly so because it is beautifully evocative. From this, he fashioned the lyric about a world where nothing is sacred and everything is for sale, and delivered it very succinctly. This is also one of his few great vocal performances on the album, particularly in the chorus which takes flight like the Maiden of old.

Musically things couldn't be more different to the previous carthorse of a track, with the band playing as if they have the wind at their heels rather than lead in their boots. Murray delivers two superb solos, one in the introduction and one towards the end, and the construction of the song is sublime. The verses lay out the view of the world in a cynical and resigned fashion, while the pre-chorus ('Nothing is sacred...') and chorus ('Judas my guide...') dovetail into each other perfectly. With such a concise running time, how this was overlooked as a single, especially in favour of 'From Here to Eternity', is beyond me. The singles charts were made for this stuff.

'Weekend Warrior' (Harris, Gers)

Another Harris-Gers co-write here, and sadly it's another fairly mundane one. The lyric this time (and we must assume this to be Harris) concerns someone who has had a gang identity as a football hooligan, and now that he no longer gains any pleasure from fighting, finds it hard to leave that identity and walk away from the pack. It's an interesting and unusual subject, tackled reasonably well, except for the fact that it is a decade too late! The prime era for organised football violence was the 1970s to early 1980s, after which the issue gradually lessened. By 1992, the arrival of all-seater stadia and general social change had left the football hooligan a relic of yesterday. Why Harris felt the need to address the issue at this point in time, is rather odd. Perhaps he will soon be penning a song about what it is like to be trapped on the wrong side of the Berlin Wall?

What of the music, though? Ah well, if the lyric is okay, but just out of time, the music is far more disappointing. The song begins with a promising acoustic guitar intro, and clumsy riffing propels the verses, with Bruce sounding for all the world as if he is either being strangled or else auditioning for AC/DC. The acoustic bits come back in every few lines for no purpose other than for the hapless Bruce to try to sound heartfelt, which the lyric can't do for him. The solos (Murray then Gers) are excellent, but another 'C minus' for songwriting, I'm afraid.

'Fear of the Dark' (Harris)

At last! Harris goes it alone, remembers how to write a song and conjures up an instant and enduring Maiden classic to close the album. The track begins with a quiet section – only this time it is a properly thought-out one. Dickinson sings the first verse and chorus in low and menacing tones over this restrained backing before the whole band burst in with one of the most recognisable lead guitar lines since 'The Trooper'. The next verse is sung to approximately the same melody, only harder and faster, and the chorus has now become immense. There is a great instrumental break, with once again Gers taking the first solo (in excellent fashion) before Murray takes over. Back to the song proper, verse, chorus, repeat, then short quiet outro echoing the beginning, and we're done. This is except for the fact that the song has taken up almost permanent residence in the stage show up to the present day, and deservedly so. It seems simple, but there are clever tricks such as subtle tempo changes in the choruses to keep it from becoming repetitive, and it is great to hear some harmony lead guitar work again.

According to Dickinson, Steve Harris was actually afraid of the dark as a child, which would certainly explain the very convincing depictions of the fear, though the song is generally believed to be also a metaphor for being afraid as an adult, only this time of uncertainty and doubt. Harris himself has commented that it is about 'being afraid, but not knowing exactly what of'.

A superlative way to end an album which has its very poor moments but overall, especially considering its greater length, is more interesting overall than *No Prayer for the Dying*. Next up though, was the end of an era, and all bets were off...

The X Factor

Personnel:
Blaze Bayley: vocals
Dave Murray: guitars
Janick Gers: guitars
Steve Harris: bass guitar
Nicko McBrain: drums
With:
Michael Kenney: keyboards
Record Label: EMI (UK), CMC (US)
Recorded: Jan-Aug 1995, produced by Nigel Green and Steve Harris
Release date: 2 October 1995
Highest chart places: UK: 8, USA: 147
Running time: 70:54

Following the *Fear of the Dark* tour, and while he had begun tentative work on his second solo album, Bruce Dickinson dropped the bombshell in 1993 that he was going to leave the band. However, the band had already booked another tour, and so he agreed to remain for the contracted dates. This proved to be a mistake, as relations between himself and Steve Harris hit an all-time low during that period. Dickinson's performances on many of the dates were undeniably far from his best, but he and Harris disagreed on the reasons. While Harris claimed that Dickinson was deliberately underperforming, and often mumbling songs, the singer denied this and claimed he had realised that he was in an impossible position as frontman when the audiences knew full well he was leaving. He claimed the atmosphere was 'like a morgue' some nights, and that not only was it difficult to perform enthusiastically under those circumstances but also he felt that if he did try to act as if everything was okay, the crowds would resent him for it anyway and that he couldn't win. When he eventually left, no-one believed that he would be back.

During 1994, the band reportedly auditioned 'hundreds' of potential singers before settling on the man Steve Harris had favoured from the start: Blaze Bayley. Born Bayley Alexander Cooke, he had been the frontman for the band Wolfsbane for ten years, until they broke up following his departure for Maiden. Shortly after joining, he was out of physical action for around a year following a serious motorcycle accident, but he was able to record vocals for the forthcoming album, so there was nothing lost. The album was again recorded in Harris's Barnyard Studios and was titled *The X Factor* because not only was it the band's tenth album, but also they felt that the material and Blaze's arrival would give it that elusive magic, or 'X Factor'.

Album Cover:

Once again, Derek Riggs was sidelined, and the band instead went for a cover design by Hugh Syme, a prolific rock sleeve artist best known for being the man behind all Rush albums from 1975's *Caress of Steel* onward. The design was a very graphic, and to some people disturbing one, featuring a very realistic image of Eddie being 'vivisected' by various machinery while strapped down. Owing to the nature of the cover, there had to be a reversible design with an alternative image showing Eddie from a distance in an electric chair. It's eye-catching to say the least, if very dark, both in tone and colour scheme. The cover to the 'Man on the Edge' single has an even more extreme close-up, which is a bit disturbing, frankly.

Things were mostly CD-driven by this time, but a double clear vinyl edition was also made available. It had a gatefold, depicting the 'distance' design on the inner spread, and also contained a poster with lyrics and photos. This was the last time until 2015 that the 'classic' Maiden logo would be used on an album, with future releases utilising a modified design truncating the extensions to the letters.

'Sign of the Cross' (Harris)

Well, this is the way to open an album and make a statement! At over eleven minutes in length, this was the longest Maiden album opener and their second-longest song after 'Ancient Mariner', and it's a genuine, dyed in the wool epic. Lyrically it is obtuse, and open to interpretation. It appears that the central character is to have his faith tested, and many have interpreted it as being a man about to face the Spanish Inquisition, but there are many unanswered questions. What is the meaning of the reference to 'The name of the rose'? It is, of course, a classic book and film concerning a medieval monk, but there seems little other connection. And who are the 'Eleven saintly shrouded men', and 'One in front with a cross held high', who have come to wash his sins away? This imagery is undoubtedly very similar to the opening to the Genesis classic 'Supper's Ready', where Peter Gabriel looks out onto his lawn and sees 'Six saintly shrouded men... A seventh walks in front, with a cross held high in hand'. Is this merely borrowing from the Genesis lyric, or are they referencing the same thing?

Perhaps it doesn't matter really, as the point of the lyric may well be for people to take what they think from it. Some of the imagery in the song is very powerful, and it is loaded with symbolism that is only accentuated by the music, which runs the whole Maiden gamut of styles. The eerie opening has Gregorian chanting which appears to be 'Aeternus Hallelujah' ('Praise the Eternal'), and this leads to a reflective couplet before the band come in with a vintage propulsive Maiden riff, followed by a big, epic chorus. The high point in many ways is the lengthy instrumental section taking up half of the song's length, which goes through echoes of all of the song's sections plus some more, and has tremendous solos from Murray and then Gers. Special mention must go to Nicko McBrain, who is astounding here, with arguably his best performance since *Powerslave*.

If a criticism can be laid it is that Bayley fails to reach the notes which would allow the chorus really to fly (a fact illustrated by the live renditions following Dickinson's return). It's not that he is bad, but he is a little lacking in range, and occasionally seems a little flat. It's a great song, but in the hands of another singer could have been greater still.

'Lord of the Flies' (Harris, Gers)

Steve Harris returns to his literary inspiration for this song, based on the novel by William Golding, about a group of schoolboys who are stranded on a deserted island and revert to a wild, uncivilised societal model. Published in 1954, it was primarily written to illustrate the 'dark side' of typical boys' adventure stories and explore the idea that the base nature within us would win out, especially in the case of children who have not yet been fully conditioned by society's accepted codes of behaviour.

Harris's lyric looks at the situation through what appears to be the viewpoint of Jack, the ex-choirboy who emerges as the de facto leader of the group and stronger than those who want to maintain a co-operative existence. Musically it is an excellent song, with the unusual construction of a lengthy 'verse' section followed by a repeated chorus, but without any overlap between the two. Opening with a choppy, jagged riff, it kicks up in tempo for the entrance of the vocal, and the verse section is enlivened by nice twists of vocal melody which lift the song above the mundane. Even Bayley is impressive on this, as he keeps well within his range and shows that when working within his limitations he has a decent, powerful voice. An excellent solo by Gers rounds off what is an excellent track. It was released as a single, but strangely not in the UK.

The title 'Lord of the Flies', incidentally, is the literal translation of 'Beelzebub', an archaic name for Satan, or 'evil personified', which is what the book theorises is dormant within us all.

'Man on the Edge' (Bayley, Gers)

Blaze Bayley gets in on the songwriting now, as he collaborates with the increasingly prolific Gers on this song based on the Michael Douglas film *Falling Down*, in which a regular white-collar worker finally snaps under the niggling stresses of everyday life. Bayley, who wrote the lyrics, should be commended for continuing the fine Maiden tradition of film and literary inspiration – this could easily have come from the Harris pen.

Musically it is fast, hard, and it simply gets in, rescues the hostages and gets out again. There's no fat in these four minutes as, apart from a deceptively slow introduction of 20 seconds or so, it rocks fast and hard with a catchy – if somewhat repetitive – chorus. It is interesting that the song is based on the film *Falling Down* and the chorus consists of just the words 'falling down' repeated over and over, yet the song is titled 'Man on the Edge'. A good title for sure, but one might have expected it to be called 'Falling Down'. Then again, the film might have been better titled 'Man on the Edge'...

The first single from the album (reaching Number Ten in the UK), it was accompanied by an official video intercutting film of the band with men falling from buildings. Falling down. Not that subtle, really.

'Fortunes of War' (Harris)

This seven-minute 'mini-epic' from Harris takes on the theme introduced in 'Afraid to Shoot Strangers', as it deals with the mental issues of soldiers returning from conflict and battling their inner demons. It's certainly less contentious than that earlier song, as there can be no accusation of political grandstanding here, just a thoughtful look at the problems faced, but often misunderstood, by returning veterans.

Musically this is very atypical for Maiden. In fact, its closest musical touchstone is some of the slower and darker Metallica songs of the time, with 'One', 'Nothing Else Matters', 'Unforgiven' and maybe even 'Sad but True' coming to mind. It opens with a very dark and mellow introduction, with Bayley doing well to sound haunted and bring out the pain inherent in the lyric. After the first verse, a slow and heavy riff comes in, with some lovely lead guitar work embroidering it, but it still doesn't do as you would expect, as it jostles for position with the quiet introductory theme for a while, both ebbing and flowing, until the heavy, chugging riff wins out for the rest of the verse. The chorus also comes in quite slowly before a superb instrumental section gives Gers and then Murray the chance to shine, before going back to a faster chorus then slowing down again, and finally, the heavy stuff abandons the fight, and the troubled 'thousand-yard stare' vocal comes back to close the song down on a dark, troubled note. This is a long, long way from 'Sanctuary' and 'Iron Maiden'.

'Look for the Truth' (Bayley, Gers, Harris)

This song – another downbeat, introspective lyric, presumably from Harris who was in a dark place personally at the time – mines a similar musical furrow as the previous track, only this time with diminishing returns. The lyric deals with a man who has buried old trauma or memories and finds them coming back to overwhelm him in the form of nightmares and dread, although he ultimately vows to overcome these shadows of the past by fighting them. The trusty slow, quiet intro is there again, but this time it is overtaken by a grinding riff which is simply rather flat and devoid of inspiration. The 'Oh-oh-oh' interludes from Bayley are dreadful, and it is hard to understand what they were thinking. There is a nice instrumental section, though the solos from Gers and then Murray are too short. Look for the truth – here it is: the song doesn't work.

'The Aftermath' (Harris, Bayley, Gers)

Another anti-war polemic from the pen of Harris proves the inspiration behind a truly excellent song, at just the point when it is needed to kick things up a notch again after 'Look for the Truth'. Indeed, there is a strong argument to remove that track from the list, as this song works perfectly when delivered right on the heels of 'Fortunes of War'.

The lyric here is certainly the best of the three recent Harris war epics ('Afraid to Shoot Strangers' being the third), as it looks at the futility and grinding horror of, particularly, the First World War. There are sentiments here which could fit any Twentieth Century conflict, for sure, but there are lyrical references which pin this one to the Western Front. The references to mustard gas and barbed wire for a start, as mustard gas was used for the first time at Passchendaele in 1917, and much less common in future conflicts after it became apparent what horrific damage it could inflict, leaving men blind or with terrible respiratory issues. There is also a lyric which talks about a farmer hitching his team of horses and seeding his land, and contrasting that with bodies strewn across the fields. The Western Front stretched right across rural France and Belgium, ripping apart the livelihoods of small farmers, and to this day bodies, rifles, helmets and unexploded bombs are still being recovered.

Of course, a great lyric doth not a great song make, but here it is backed up by excellent musical accompaniment – some of which may take time to grow, as this is no immediate 'Trooper' or 'Run to the Hills', but grow it will. Opening with a beautifully atmospheric intro with delicate percussion from Nicko and some sensitive guitar work from Gers, it soon slams into a juddering verse riff which is not dissimilar to a heavier Wishbone Ash (see their song 'Warrior', for example). After two verses and quite similar choruses, the song shifts into a new section with a litany of 'After the War' observations, which initially seems plodding but is, in fact, perfectly judged. The line 'I'm just a soldier' leads into a sudden hell-for-leather instrumental section with a coruscating solo from Janick Gers, doing some of his best Maiden work here. Another 'After the War' section and we're done.

A mature and thoughtful song delivered without giving in to the easy option of the old Maiden 'gallop' – another highlight on this very underrated album.

'Judgement of Heaven' (Harris)

This one is a real oddity, seeming to fall between two stools yet managing to straddle the gap pretty well. The lyric here is simultaneously dark and yet uplifting. Harris talks about how depressed he has been for so long, and how many times he has thought of suicide, and also implores God to tell him if things will ever get better, will he ever rest in peace. So far so grim (this is one of the songs which really does show the dark place Harris was in personally when making this album), but by the same token he also states that taking one's own life would be the 'easy way', the 'selfish way', and that the hardest thing is to 'get on with your life'. I have read many testimonials from people who have stated that this lyric, and the delivery of those first few lines by Bayley, has been instrumental in giving them the inner strength they needed, and I can understand how this could be the case. Musically the song is very bass-driven and opens with pumping, fat bass driving the vocals. The band come in and, at first, it seems a little pedestrian, but the tempo gradually picks up and seems to lift the mood as it does. The final choruses of 'All of my life I have believed, judgement of heaven is waiting for me' are magnificent, and in fact, in this case, do not need any of Bruce's high notes and operatic magnificence – it's just perfect as it is. Only a few years after this was released, Dream Theater would put out their conceptual classic *Scenes From A Memory*, and it is easy to imagine them listening to this and gaining inspiration both musically and lyrically for 'The Spirit Carries On', and one or two more. A quiet little classic this one, almost hiding in plain sight.

'Blood on the World's Hands' (Harris)
It's the horrors of war again at the hands of a seemingly obsessed Harris, but in fact, this sounds very fresh, even at a point when 'war fatigue' could be setting in a little. The subject here (though it isn't explicit) is the Balkan conflict in the mid-'90s, a subject rarely covered in rock music (for an additional listen, see the concept album *Dead Winter Dead* by Savatage, which covers this conflict in unerring detail and powerful accuracy).

What makes this song unique by even Maiden's progressive leanings is the juddering stop-start momentum of the verses, along with a vocal melody going against the riff yet somehow working with it – it is like nothing so much as a heavier Gentle Giant, and it is quite spellbinding. The chorus is also notable, as is the sudden ending of 'Someone should...', leaving the statement hanging. The solos, by Murray followed by Gers, are again excellent, and in truth the only thing going against this one is the rather too lengthy jazzy bass intro from Harris (well over a minute) which doesn't fit, to be honest. It's a fine song, though.

'The Edge of Darkness' (Harris, Bayley, Gers)
Back to the film-and-literature inspiration here, while still keeping a foot in that war-themed camp, as this is directly about the film *Apocalypse Now,* set in the Vietnam War, which in itself is based on the Joseph Conrad novel *Heart of Darkness*. The film, for those who haven't seen it, concerns a trip up-river by a man (Captain Willard) sent to kill a renegade Green Beret (Colonel Kurtz) who has given way to savagery and set himself up as a god among a local tribe. The lyrics largely consist of almost direct quotes from the film, so being familiar with it certainly help in this case.

It's another decent song, going through several moods, from slow atmospheric opening to up-and down-tempo sections, with once again a good instrumental section with solos from Gers then Murray. The only negative is that there is a slight sense of 'nothing new here', as the song relies on several tropes already established on the album for its template. One could ask how many more slow, brooding intros do we need, and the trick of speeding up and slowing back down again is becoming rather familiar. It's well-executed, has a great lyrical idea and a good vocal performance from Blaze – but perhaps just a sense of '*X Factor* by numbers' creeping in. Then again, part of that problem is the overlong album, which really should have had some tighter editing.

'2 AM' (Bayley, Gers, Harris)

Steve 'Mr Happy' Harris gets in touch with his inner misery again on this rumination on the futility of life, as seen through the eyes of a late-night worker living on his own who gets in from work at 2 AM to the company of beer, TV and desperate existential angst. It's fairly slight lyrically, In fact, with only two four-line verses and the rest being a repeated chorus and an instrumental section. Once again, we have the slow, reflective opening, reprised at the end, and the big, slow, grinding chords accompanying the chorus. It's okay for what it is, being close to what you might call a 'power ballad', with the emphasis on 'power', but there isn't a lot here melodically and Bayley sounds a bit flat, especially in the chorus. One thing Bruce did have over Blaze is that, on the occasion that there would be a song without a lot of distinctive melody, he'd try to give it a little more vocal character. Blaze, by contrast, just sings it straight here, which is a bit, well, dull. Nice solo from Janick, mind you.

This track highlights as well as any what the main flaw is with this admittedly underrated album. It departs significantly from the old Maiden template of the galloping riff and the big choruses, but ironically, the darker, slower-paced format it uses soon becomes over-familiar in itself. So ironically, the album is different yet too samey. Maiden have gone through the motions at times before, but these motions aren't always as good...

'The Unbeliever' (Harris, Gers)

A long (eight-minute) track to close the album, this has some similarities lyrically with 'Judgement of Heaven', being an introspective song with feelings of depression and self-loathing not far beneath the surface of the central character. It's okay but perhaps we've reached one downbeat lyric too far. Musically it isn't the best either, to be honest, with the 'prog stakes' being upped a little with the atonal guitar and tricky time signature of the verses without real success and the chorus also, like the previous song, never really taking off, with Bayley saving one of his worst performances on the album until last. There is also a mercifully short yet horrible part at the beginning (and repeated later) which effectively sounds as if they are tuning up. Overall there's a general feeling of trying something brave which doesn't quite come off. Things speed up after the instrumental and the song gets a little bit of a belated kick, and there is one moment of genius when Dave Murray's solo starts, transitioning directly out of Janick's solo brilliantly, but it's too little too late to save an undistinguished climax to the record. Iron Maiden are and have always been a great band, but they are not, and never will be, King Crimson.

Related songs:

'Virus' (Harris, Gers, Murray, Bayley)

Released as a single after the X Factor tour had finished, this song is generally accepted to have been written as a barbed response to the fierce criticism they, and Bayley in particular, had received. The song is rather unusual for Maiden.

Firstly, it is the first single not to appear on any studio album since 'Women In Uniform' , but it also happens to be the only song of theirs with writing credits for both Murray and Gers, discounting two band-credited jams. Six minutes long, the first part is quite dynamic, with the old slow intro trick and interspersed bursts of staccato riffing in between the moody verses. When it then explodes into an anticipated fast 'gallop', the effect may be a hackneyed trick, but it is undeniably a powerful one. The instrumental section does drag a little toward the end. An opportunistic two-part CD release had rather pointless covers of UFO's 'Doctor Doctor' and The Who's 'My Generation' on one part, with the old Metal For Muthas tracks on the other.

'Judgement Day' (Bayley, Gers)
Left off the album but used on the 'Man on the Edge' single, this is an absolutely balls-out, thunderbolt rocker, coming out of the traps at 100mph and never letting up. Murray and Gers (then Murray again) let rip with a series of astonishing solos, and the whole thing has a joy and exhilaration about it which would really have given the album a burst or adrenalin it could sorely have used. At least three songs could have made way for this to produce a better album

Lyrically there isn't too much going on, just a general air of there being no way to tell by a person's appearance what sort of character they are, and that we will all atone on the day of judgement.

'I Live My Way' (Harris, Bayley, Gers)
A real rarity, this track, as it can only be found on the picture disc of the 'Man on the Edge' single – and also a Japanese special edition of the album. The intro is beautiful, but it then descends into a forgettable, plodding rocker with monotonous Bayley vocals and a clumsy lyric about wanting to live your life how you want to, which comes across as a bit petulant, actually. This one was well left off the main album.

'Justice of the Peace' (Murray, Harris)
From the 'Part 2' of the 'Man on the Edge' single, which was an appalling packaging rip-off, sharing two identical album tracks with 'Part 1'. This is a rather run-of-the-mill rocker with only some nice guitar licks in the chorus and a decent solo from Murray lifting it above the norm. It still could have a case argued for it being on the album, though not as strongly as 'Judgement Day'.

The lyrics are awful, yet amusing in a 'so bad they're good' way, as Harris laments the rise of the criminal element in society. A decent sentiment, but the way he does it uses every old cliché in the book: 'throw the book at them', 'in my day nobody locked their doors, but there was no trouble' and even, at one point, the hoary old 'we didn't have much money, but we were happy'. You almost expect a chorus of orphans from *Oliver Twist* to come looming up in the chorus...

Virtual XI

Personnel:
Blaze Bayley: vocals
Dave Murray: guitars
Janick Gers: guitars
Steve Harris: bass guitar, keyboards
Nicko McBrain: drums
With:
Michael Kenney: keyboards
Record Label: EMI (UK), CMC (US)
Recorded: late 1997-Feb 1998, produced by Nigel Green and Steve Harris
Release date: 23 March 1998
Highest chart places: UK: 16, USA: 124
Running time: 53:22

The second and final album with Blaze Bayley was a confused and unfocused affair, lacking the sense of direction of *The X Factor*. It did, however, sidestep that album's worst failings by being less morose in tone, and also shorter – although the songs are fewer and individually longer. By the time of this release, fans had begun to turn against Blaze Bayley in greater numbers after he disappointed in the live environment, especially on the Dickinson songs – and indeed, a number of US dates had to be cancelled after he had troubles with his voice. The official reason given for this at the time was allergies – which fooled no-one. It is generally accepted now that his voice was feeling the strain of having to try to sing outside his range. This is not his fault, of course, and it indicates that perhaps he should have been auditioned in greater depth with the material he would have to perform on stage. He had this second bite at the cherry, in any case.

  One reason for the unfocused feel of the release is the fact that it was heavily influenced by two outside events, one being the release of the *Ed Hunter* Maiden computer game, and the other being the World Cup in France in 1998. The former led to the designs for the album booklet almost all coming from the game, together with the 'Virtual' part of the title. This diminished the album somewhat to the status of perceived 'video game tie-in', something unthinkable when the album releases were such major events in the previous decades. The whole World Cup thing, leading to the 'XI' part of the title and much of the packaging, was even more tangential, as Harris reasoned (with flawed logic, I may add) that most of the band's fans would share their interests and hobbies. As he said, in Mick Wall's biography of the group, *Run to the Hills*, 'We figure our fans are pretty much the same as we are, with pretty much the same interests, so we thought, "It's World Cup year in '98. Let's get the football involved in the new album". And we were already working on a computer game at that time, so we thought, "Well, let's bring that element into things, too"'. This sort of chucking everything topical at the album had never been done before and was a mistake. Many very keen music fans don't share anything like that passion for sport, and the link between football and the target video game demographic is even more dubious, and it was frankly presumptuous on the part of Harris to assume that their audience would mirror their interests merely because they enjoy the music. I mean, okay, I like football, beer and computer games, so I may be undermining my own argument, but I wouldn't set myself up as a model, either. In fact, continuing with the football theme, the band did a publicity tour before release wherein they organised football matches across Europe against guest opponents, which is an odd thing to do. Even worse, the programme for the following world tour would feature a front cover with a ghastly picture of Eddie as a footballer, in shorts, kicking the earth. Oh, dear.

The album was again recorded at Harris's Barnyard Studio but was the last one the band would do there.

Album Cover:

Hugh Syme was not asked back for this one, so there are no graphic images of Eddie being tortured to feast one's eyes on this time out. Instead, the cover is from Melvyn Grant again, who should really have been kept on following his excellent *Fear of the Dark* art, but that's by the way. The front cover of this one is a pretty effective illustration of a kid playing what appears to be a virtual reality game, while Eddie appears as a terrifying demonic creature from another reality, about to grab him. Unless, of course, the Eddie figure is a part of the game he is playing and is the virtual reality he is seeing. It can be interpreted either way, but it's quite eye-catching anyhow. Less successful is the seemingly random inclusion of a football game taking place in the distance. Grant has said that he had to add that in because, while he was initially asked just to do something with a VR feel to it, he was asked later to put something football-related in there as a part of the band's seemingly obsessive World Cup idea.

The booklet contains a lot of imagery from the forthcoming *Ed Hunter* video game, which has unsurprisingly quickly dated and was a poor idea from the start. In addition to these game images, and the lyrics, a photo spread in the booklet shows the band lining up as part of an Iron Maiden football team. Accompanying the band as part of the team in the photo are actual professional footballers Stuart Pearce, Faustino Asprilla, Paul Gascoigne, Ian Wright, Patrick Viera and Marc Overmars. Oddly, none of these were West Ham players.

There was a vinyl release of the album, strangely enough, a double album, even though it is only 53-minutes long. There are inner sleeves with photos and lyrics, while the inner gatefold shows the Iron Maiden football team photo again.

'Futureal' (Harris, Bayley)

Back to the days of the short, sharp, fast-paced album opener, and no bad thing for that. It's fairly simplistic and only lasts three minutes – which may well be Maiden's shortest non-instrumental track – but it gets the blood pumping and gets the album going right out of the blocks. It's not a great song in itself, with a somewhat weak chorus, and I'm not sure about the wisdom of making it a single, but it works as an opener. The solo is by Murray – the whole instrumental section is the best part of the song.

The lyrics have often been claimed to be about someone becoming obsessed with on-line video gaming and losing sight of what is real, but that isn't strictly true. Bayley, who wrote the lyric to the music Harris already had, confirms that it is actually about the paranoia of misinformation in this media-overloaded modern world, with the powers that be having the ability to make you think what they want you to think. Or maybe they've just made me think that...

'The Angel and the Gambler' (Harris)

Oh my, they really stirred up a hornet's nest with this one! Despite being the first single from the album, this is, without doubt, one of the most disliked Maiden songs within their fanbase. The prime reason for this is the chorus repetition which, even for a band who have been guilty of this more than once, is extreme here. By the time Blaze has asked 'Don't you think I could save your life' for the umpteenth time, there is a temptation to reply with 'Yes, just end this song already and we're good'. There are good moments here, but they are far too few for a song clocking in at just shy of ten minutes. The instrumental section, with Murray then Gers delivering excellent solos, is the brightest moment, and the chorus is very good for perhaps the first three or four times. Once you get past twenty, it's wearing extremely thin. There are also some horrible-sounding keyboard parts which deserve a dishonourable mention. On the face of it, the song is merely a story about an inveterate gambler and an angel who tries, unsuccessfully, to save him from himself. It is likely, however, that there is an intentional double meaning, with the gambling being a metaphor for making right or wrong choices in one's life. Repeating that chorus a thousand times was definitely one of those 'wrong choices'. The aforementioned keyboard additions are supplied by Steve Harris on this particular track as well, which would count as another wrong choice from the sound of them.

'Lightning Strikes Twice' (Murray, Harris)

Another slightly weak entry here, with a lyric which describes the approaching of a coming storm, although it may well have a deeper metaphorical meaning, judging by the references to 'it happening again' and the appeals to God. Either that, or the guy has a serious fear of lightning.

Musically this is up and down. It begins with a lovely introduction, but like some of the *X Factor* album, this shifts from a nice reflective vocal beginning to a sledgehammer slow part. And rinse and repeat again. Things pick up as we approach the two-minute mark with a great up-tempo riff not dissimilar to Hawkwind's 'Master of the Universe', and this gives the track a real powerful, driving feel, almost as if the thunder and the torrential rain have arrived. Sadly, the chorus (well, eight repetitions of 'Maybe lightning strikes twice' if that counts as a chorus) is very poor, and like so many Maiden songs, certainly from this era, there is no chorus until three-quarters of the way through the track, and then there is nothing else, apart from an adequate instrumental section, which is fast and energetic, but sees Murray and then Gers 'phoning it in' somewhat.

Lightning struck with '2 AM' and 'Angel and the Gambler'. This one takes the worst traits of those two and reuses them. So yes, it can strike twice, unfortunately.

'The Clansman' (Harris)

Inspired by the 1995 films *Braveheart* and *Rob Roy*, this clear highpoint of the album is probably the only real enduring classic to come from the Bayley era (along with, possibly, 'Sign of the Cross' in terms of live songs). This time around everything that the previous two songs got wrong is done absolutely right. There are quiet parts, loud parts, fast parts, slow parts and a big stirring chorus, but every building block fits together perfectly to make a masterpiece. The instrumental section has some nice Celtic flavours in it, and the solos by Gers and then Murray are top quality. Even Bayley does okay on this one, when normally it would be too much for him to sound too uplifting. It certainly sounds as if all concerned know this is great stuff and are totally committed to it. Harris handles the keyboards here, and he acquits himself well on this occasion.

One has to say, however, that although Blaze makes a good fist of this, the subsequent live versions with the returning Dickinson take things to another level entirely, and give the song its true justice. The sight of Bruce waving a huge Scottish flag while thousands of people roar 'Freedom!' in unison with him is not easily forgotten. This song, and also 'Sign of the Cross', were true highlights of the *Brave New World* tour a couple of years after this album.

'When Two Worlds Collide' (Murray, Bayley, Harris)

Another pretty good song, this one is mostly written by Murray and Bayley. Harris himself has admitted that 'Dave wrote most of the music and Blaze wrote the lyrics', while he added some parts and arranged the song. Lyrically it is about an approaching asteroid or comet found to be approaching Earth on a collision course. Some have suggested there is a secondary meaning, concerning when two cultures collide, such as the Europeans and the Native Americans, but this is probably reading too much into it. The lyric specifically references telescopes, computers, stars and a speck of light getting bigger as it approaches. Sometimes a song is just a song.

The verses and chorus are both very good, with strong melodies throughout, while the solos from Murray and then Gers are both excellent, with Murray taking the clear honours this time out with his brilliant excursion around the fretboard. It's certainly a very creditable song, though once again is marred slightly by that habit of having all the verse lines front-loaded with the entire second half being instrumental and multiple choruses. Lyrically, it is unbalanced, to say the least.

One special mention has to go to Blaze Bayley here, for firstly managing to use the word 'declination' in a song lyric, but then going on to heroically rhyme it with 'calculations'. Take a bow sir, your place in lyrical history is assured...

'The Educated Fool' (Harris)

Another contemplative lyric from Harris, who really does seem to be undergoing some sort of mid-life crisis at this point, from the point of view of a man who seems to have reached a point when he realises he wants more from his life, and to achieve more of his potential. The lyrics are occasionally rather clumsy ('As I'm walking down into / On my own into the valley of life' and 'could this just be that life's just begun', not to mention the odd use of the word 'respond' in 'I want to feel what life's like respond'), but the overall thoughtful quality of the song makes these more forgivable. There are a couple of lines hinting at a secondary meaning, such as 'Seems that somebody's just opened the door to the book of life – or is it death?' and also 'I want to meet my father beyond' (Steve's father had notably died not long before this), so it is certainly a song on which to transfer one's own interpretation.

Musically this is excellent. The instrumental section (with two magnificent solos from Murray and then an equally fired up Gers) is fast and hard, but overall this isn't really a metal song at all. It is filtered slightly through the Maiden template, but it's really a musically diverse and mature song which just happens to be wearing a bullet belt.

'Don't Look to the Eyes of a Stranger' (Harris)

This song has Steve Harris looking at a violent crime through the victim's eyes, as a sort of reversal of *Killers*, where it was from the attacker's viewpoint. It's a multi-faceted song musically, though not entirely successfully, as the various parts, covering slow and heavy, fast and heavy, mid-paced and almost orchestral, feel somewhat bolted together, as if it's more a collection of ideas strung together than a song. Even the speedy instrumental section with decent solos from Gers then Murray is an odd fit, as it seems to pick up its heels and clip along in a rather jolly manner, which doesn't exactly scream 'Stranger Danger!' as people happily bounce up and down.

Lyrically this seems to have come down with a nasty dose of 'Angel and the Gambler', as the words 'Don't look to' are repeated so many times they almost lose all meaning. I mean, the song is over eight minutes long and vocal-led almost throughout, and there are precisely eight – count them, eight – lines which don't start with the words 'Don't look to'. We get it, we won't look. We probably won't listen too often either, to be honest.

'Como Estais Amigos' (Bayley, Gers)

This song, about the Argentine people with regard to the Falklands conflict, is supposedly intended to mean 'How are you, friends'. It doesn't. That would be

'Como estas'. 'Como estais amigos' actually translates as 'since you are friends', as in for example, 'since you are friends, we can talk to you'. Which might be intended, who knows?

Whatever, it's a good song to close the album. With an excellent Bayley lyric pleading for the lessons to be learned and the sadness and horror never to return, the song moves from a solemn beginning into a full band affair – albeit still with the same solemnity – midway through the second verse. In fact, the opening verse and chorus are so good that this could easily have been done straight like that throughout, and left as a moving ballad, but one suspects that the band didn't quite have the confidence to go so far down that particular rabbit hole at this time. The only complaint might be the solo from Gers (who wrote the music), which would have been more effective had it fit better with the mood of the song – instead, it sounds just a little generic, and as a result jars slightly.

It has a good vocal performance from Bayley, though, and a great vocal melody in the chorus, so he manages to go out on something of a high.

There are no related songs, as the single releases from the album all used live versions of existing tracks as B-sides.

Above: Steve Harris, in typical pose onstage. (*Alamy*)

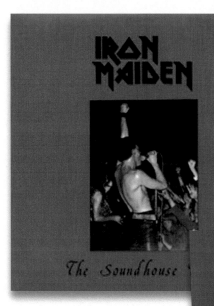

Left: *The Soundhouse Tapes*, the three-track EP which was the first Iron Maiden release - named for the venue where it was first regularly played. (*Rock Hard Records*)

Right: The rear cover of *The Soundhouse Tapes*, with notes by Neal Kay, DJ at the Soundhouse venue. (*Rock Hard Records*)

Left: *Live!! + One*, a live EP released in Japan in 1980. (*EMI*)

Right: Paul Diano, Freedom Hall, Johnson City, Tennessee, July 10th, 1981 on the 'Killers' tour, where the band opened for Judas Priest. (*Photo: Bryan Cline*)

Left: Adrian Smith in Tennessee, again on the 'Killers' tour. (*Photo: Bryan Cline*)

Right: One final shot from Tennessee on the 'Killers' tour, this time featuring Steve Harris. (*Photo: Bryan Cline*)

Left: The self-titled debut album, 1980. (*EMI*)

Right: The *Killers* album in 1981 - Adrian Smith's debut. (*EMI*)

Left: The provocative cover to the 'Women In Uniform' single, notable for the appearance of a cartoon Margaret Thatcher (British Prime Minister at the time) in an army uniform and carrying a firearm. (*EMI*)

Right: The game-changing *Number Of The Beast* album, from 1982. It was Bruce Dickinson's debut, of course. (*EMI*)

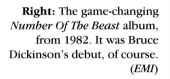

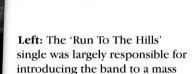

Left: The 'Run To The Hills' single was largely responsible for introducing the band to a mass audience. (*EMI*)

Right: *Piece Of Mind* (1983), on which Nicko McBrain made his first appearance on drums. (*EMI*)

Left: Bruce Dickinson at the Huntington Civic Center, Huntington, West Virginia, September 28th, 1982 on the 'Beast On The Road' tour, again supporting Judas Priest. (*Photo: Bryan Cline*)

Right: Dave Murray and Dickinson, again in Huntington, West Virginia, September 28th, 1982 on the the 'Beast On The Road' tour. (*Photo: Bryan Cline*)

Left: Dave Murray again at the Huntington Civic Center in 1982. (*Photo: Bryan Cline*)

Right: Steve Harris (with Eddie) at the Huntington Civic Center, Huntington, West Virginia, September 28th, 1982 on the 'Beast On The Road' tour. (*Photo: Bryan Cline*)

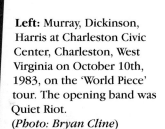

Left: Murray, Dickinson, Harris at Charleston Civic Center, Charleston, West Virginia on October 10th, 1983, on the 'World Piece' tour. The opening band was Quiet Riot. (*Photo: Bryan Cline*)

Right: Murray, Smith, Harris (and a hideous Eddie) again at Charleston Civic Center in 1983, on the 'World Piece' tour. (*Photo: Bryan Cline*)

Left: Paul Di'Anno, singing 'Remember Tomorrow' on German TV.

Right: A still from the 'Run To The Hills' video, featuring Murray, Harris and Smith.

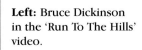

Left: Bruce Dickinson in the 'Run To The Hills' video.

Right: Still from the 'Can I Play With Madness' video, featuring an almost unrecognisable Graham Chapman of Monty Python fame.

Left: Another still from the 'Can I Play With Madness' video.

Right: A still from the bizarre, yet amusing, 'Holy Smoke' video.

Left: The immensely successful *Powerslave* album from 1984. (*EMI*)

Right: The *Somewhere In Time* album, 1986 - the front and back covers were full of in-jokes and Maiden references. (*EMI*)

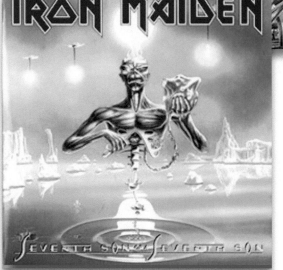

Left: *Seventh Son Of A Seventh Son*, 1988 - the last album to feature the 'classic' five-piece line-up. (*EMI*)

Right: *No Prayer For The Dying*, 1990 - on which Janick Gers made his Maiden debut. (*EMI*)

Left: *Fear Of The Dark*, 1992 - after which Bruce Dickinson took his (temporary) leave. (*EMI*)

Right: *The X Factor* and its hideous cover, 1995 - with Blaze Bayley making his first appearance. (*EMI*)

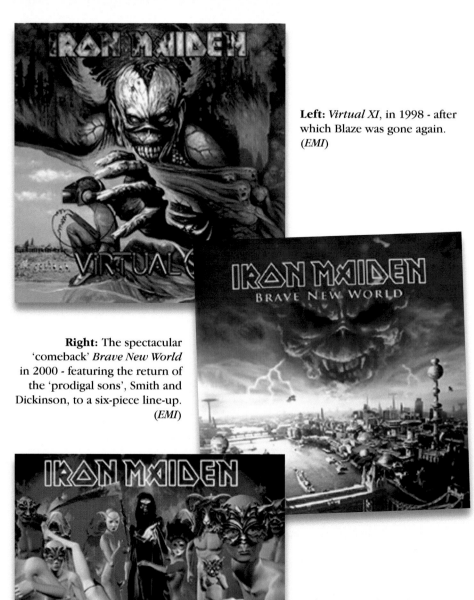

Left: *Virtual XI*, in 1998 - after which Blaze was gone again. (*EMI*)

Right: The spectacular 'comeback' *Brave New World* in 2000 - featuring the return of the 'prodigal sons', Smith and Dickinson, to a six-piece line-up. (*EMI*)

Left: *Dance Of Death*, 2003 - a cover design generally regarded as 'unfortunate', to put it mildly. (*EMI*)

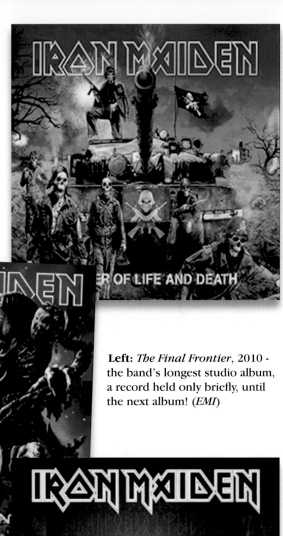

Right: *A Matter Of Life And Death*, 1986 - with an army of undead Eddies. (*EMI*)

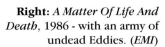

Left: *The Final Frontier*, 2010 - the band's longest studio album, a record held only briefly, until the next album! (*EMI*)

Right: *The Book Of Souls*, 2015 - Maiden's first studio double album, and the most recent at time of publication. (*Parlophone*)

Above: Live in Santiago, Chile, 2011 - group shot.

Below: Live in Santiago, Chile, 2011 - Dave Murray.

Above: Live in Santiago, Chile, 2011 - Murray, Smith, Gers.

Below: Live in Santiago, Chile, 2011 - Nicko McBrain in alarming close-up.

Left: Janick Gers' first ever vinyl appearance with White Spirit, 1980. Note misspelling, as the song is 'Back To The Grind'. (*Author's collection*)

Right: Bruce Dickinson somehow found time at the turn of the '90s to write two entertaining comedic novels featuring his 'Lord Iffy Boatrace' character. Nobody knows how! (*Author's collection*)

Left: Blaze Bayley. Often the 'forgotten man' of Iron Maiden, but he steadied the ship when it could have run aground in the 1990s.

Brave New World

Personnel:
Bruce Dickinson: vocals
Dave Murray: guitars
Janick Gers: guitars
Adrian Smith: guitars
Steve Harris: bass guitar, keyboards
Nicko McBrain: drums
Record Label: EMI (UK), Portrait/Columbia (US)
Recorded: Oct 1999-April 2000, produced by Kevin Shirley and Steve Harris
Release date: 29 May 2000
Highest chart places: UK: 7, USA: 39
Running time: 66:57

All Change – again. This time, however, in an entirely positive way. In the last line-up change up to the time of writing (the most stable Maiden line-up ever, lasting an amazing 20 years – the same length of time as from the debut album to this point in 1999).

Following the *Virtual XI* world tour, Blaze Bayley was dismissed in a band meeting. His performances on the tour had not been good enough, and as on the previous jaunt, his vocal problems caused several cancelled shows. At the same time, Bruce Dickinson, having released a string of excellent solo albums during his time away, had indicated he might be ready for a return. It was, effectively, a no-brainer, as they say. Steve Harris has always claimed he was against it at first until he was convinced of the wisdom, but it is hard to believe even for a minute that he would look a gift horse like this in the mouth. True, they had personal issues towards the end of Bruce's first tenure, but happily, the hatchet was well and truly buried when the reformation occurred.

Perhaps even less predictable was the simultaneous return of Adrian Smith, absent for two albums longer than Dickinson, who few thought would ever return to a Maiden stage. Looking behind the curtain a little, however, reveals this to be a logical move. Smith's band Psycho Motel (not a household name, shall we say) had actually supported Maiden on the British leg of their *X Factor* tour, and after that he joined Bruce Dickinson's band full-time, appearing on the albums *Accident of Birth* and *The Chemical Wedding* and taking part in two world tours, so he had moved closer to the Maiden orbit than some had perhaps realised.

In many ways, the element of this reshuffle which is the most surprising, even looking back now, is that Janick Gers was retained. On hearing that Smith was coming back, he must surely have begun mentally packing his bags and maybe wondering whether a White Spirit reunion might happen, but the band – and particularly Harris – showed commendable loyalty in retaining him as part of a very unusual six-man, three-guitar line-up. Try to think about how many bands, particularly metal bands, have six members without one being a keyboard player. It's a short list. However, it has been proven to be a shrewd move time and again since then.

Since Martin Birch had retired from production duties, Nigel Green had handled co-production with Harris at Barnyard Studios, but Dickinson was adamant that not only should they engage a higher profile producer but also that they should head out of the barn into a proper studio again. As part of this 'brave new world' idea, Harris agreed and the band headed to Guillaume Tell Studios, Paris, along with producer Kevin Shirley, who had already worked with such acts as Rush, Journey, Dream Theater, Aerosmith and The Black Crowes over the previous decade or so.

Before recording, the band embarked on a relatively short tour covering the US and Canada, as well as mainland Europe, called the *Ed Hunter* Tour. No new material was premiered at those shows, but most of the material for the album had already been at least partly written before it commenced. Smith has claimed that three of the album's tracks, 'The Nomad', 'Dream of Mirrors' and 'Mercenary', were originally intended for *Virtual XI*, but not used. In fact, Bayley has insisted that he wrote some lyrics for 'Dream of Mirrors' but was not credited. Harris also maintains that 'Blood Brothers' was partly worked on at that time, but not finished.

Album Cover:

Derek Riggs is back! Well, partly, at least. The front cover, depicting Eddie's face in ominous storm clouds looking down at a futuristic London, is actually a collaboration between Riggs, who did the top half with Eddie, and digital artist Steve Stone, who contributed the reimagined London landscape. It's an unusual idea, but it works very well, as the resulting powerful image is arguably Maiden's strongest cover since the 1980s, with the vibrant purple/blue colouring jumping from the picture. The rear cover isn't so impressive, showing the band standing together, looking up as if in awe at the tracklisting above their heads – well, all apart from Gers and Smith over on the left of shot, who look rather embarrassed at the whole thing. There was a vinyl release, though on a much smaller scale than the CD, as this was a low ebb for the 12" format at the time. It was the expected double LP and gatefold, with the length of CD albums making this mostly unavoidable, and most of the somewhat unremarkable CD booklet design is used for the inner gatefold and inner sleeves.

'The Wicker Man' (Smith, Harris, Dickinson)

It's not too much of an exaggeration to say that the moment they heard the opening to this track, swathes of Maiden fans breathed a sigh of relief and thought 'That's what we've been missing!', because there is an indefinable quality to this song that the Bayley albums somehow lacked. Ironically, it has 'the X factor'.

Opening with a steam-hammer-fast riff which harks right back to 'Aces High', Dickinson immediately shows that his voice is far better than it had been during his last couple of albums with the band. His voice had been in top shape during his solo hiatus also, so it may well reflect a real confidence in the material he is singing. Familiar Maiden tropes are present here – a 'pre-chorus' ('You watch the world exploding every single night') which is very strong in itself, but only preparing us for the mighty main chorus of 'Your time will come', which raises the proverbial roof. The lyrics are quite opaque, and open to interpretation, but they do not directly reference the film *The Wicker Man* – Dickinson has said that it is called that as a nod to the movie because the phrase is mentioned in the lyric, but that there is no further connection. Note that Dickinson had recorded a track called 'Wicker Man' during the sessions for his album *Accident of Birth* which does reference the film more overtly. The song crept out on the bonus second disc of his *The Best of Bruce Dickinson* compilation.

The track is not perfect – the chorus is repeated just a little too much, while the closing 'whoa-oa' section is redundant and should have been cut, and also the solo by Smith rambles on somewhat and could be far better – but overall this is a real feeling of 'we've got Maiden back again'. It was the first single, preceding the album by three weeks, and made Number Nine in the UK chart. Derek Riggs did some stunning artwork for the single sleeve, but for some bizarre reason, it was rejected, with terrible band photos (a flaming torch!) and a good-but-inferior Mark Wilkinson design used instead on most versions.

'Ghost of the Navigator' (Gers, Dickinson, Harris)

Things go from good to better with this superlative seafaring song, in the fine tradition of 'Rime of the Ancient Mariner'. It's a metaphor for life, with Dickinson explaining that the navigators are ourselves with the 'ghosts' being our aspirations and things we have failed to accomplish, which try to derail us like the Sirens of legend. It's a great lyric and shows once again what an underrated wordsmith Bruce Dickinson has always been. The song opens with a quiet intro, which begins slowly, building up as drums start to enter the picture, slashing guitar chords heightening the tension before it gets released with a cathartic Gers riff which churns along like the finest vintage Sabbath, and powers the verse relentlessly. A short 'mid-section' ('Mysteries of time...') seems to cast about, adrift in search of a melody, before the mighty pre-chorus of 'I see ghosts of navigators...' comes crashing through like the bow of a mighty ship triumphantly cresting a vast wave. It's a magnificent moment, and one repeated after each verse, leading into the huge main chorus, 'Take my heart and set it free...', which uplifts and lightens the spirit. Marvellous, marvellous stuff.

Gers takes the solo here, in splendid fashion, and the whole thing goes by in almost seven minutes which seem like three. Bruce is back on full, multi-octave power here, and with all respect to Blaze Bayley, who brought what he had to the party, Iron Maiden has found its voice again, both literally and figuratively. With Gers supplying most of the music here, and Harris adding a section after the fact, it is clear that the band now have an array of songwriting talent that they have never had before.

'Brave New World' (Murray, Harris, Dickinson)

If 'The Wicker Man' was not directly about the book forming the title's inspiration, 'Brave New World' certainly is. Written by Aldous Huxley in 1932, it is a 'dystopian future' tale, in a similar vein to the better known *1984*, albeit predating that book by some fifteen years. In *Brave New World* the advent of the modern world can be easily discerned, with the population kept dosed and docile by a drug called Soma, and entertainment and experiences provided by full-sensory 'movies' known as 'feelies', which can be touched and smelt as well as seen and heard. It is presented as a sort of Utopia, as all war, famine and disease have been eliminated, although this is at the expense of emotion, free will and diversity. The central character (the 'savage') rebels against all of this and ends up seen as some kind of outcast circus freak.

Dickinson does a creditable job of distilling this landmark work down to just twelve verse lines, and the music is the equal of his words. A gentle beginning continues through the first verse, with the three guitars working brilliantly in unison, spinning a kind of web of sound behind the singer. As the full band enter for the second half of the verse, there is an argument that the vocal melody is a little weak, but that is immediately forgotten as the massive chorus bursts in. The tempos of the song work superbly here, as the verse speeds up to the chorus, which again speeds up to a double tempo second verse, which brakes suddenly into another chorus of the same pace as the first, but somehow appearing slower and more anthemic owing to the use of the changing tempo. A lightning-fast instrumental section featuring blistering solos by Gers and then Murray gives way to that fist-punching chorus again. The moment of pure genius here is halfway through each chorus when the words change subtly from 'A brave new world / In a brave new world' to 'In a brave new world / A brave new world' and just at that point, Bruce shifts up an octave. The effect is stunning every time. Roll over Blaze Bayley and tell Paul Di'Anno the news, Bruce is back – and how!

'Blood Brothers' (Harris)

The classics keep on coming as Steve Harris contributes his first solo writing contribution of the album with this acknowledged masterpiece. Lyrically it is among his best, as he appeals for an end to the folly, greed and conflict of life, insisting that – as he has said himself – 'we are all made of bone and tissue', so we are all essentially blood brothers. It's a simple yet very powerful image. There is also a mention of his late father, who he thinks of before the memory is gone (a reflection in a stream) and 'the wounds reopen again'. At that point, it seems that there is a double meaning, and he and his father are forever blood brothers.

The verses are all reflective and very bass-driven, with no temptation to break into a clichéd 'gallop', until the simple chorus – just the words 'We're blood brothers' repeated – which is so huge and passionately delivered by Dickinson that it seems to be at once life-affirming and, after the lines about Steve's father, heart-breaking. As the song develops, after Dave Murray's solo, a Celtic feel creeps in and Janick's solo is absolutely masterful as he channels that feeling and brings it into his playing. The song has orchestration by American keyboard player, composer and arranger Jeff Bova, which works perfectly to combine with the guitars to produce the Celtic overtones.

Special mention must go to the live performances of this song when it was debuted on the *Brave New World* tour, with the chorus uniting band and audience in triumphant harmony every night. Stunning.

'The Mercenary' (Gers, Harris)

The first hint of a misstep on the album, this is a perfectly acceptable fast Maiden rocker, but it's nothing more than that. Nice riff and lightning-fast solos from Smith (especially) and Murray, but compared to the bar set by the previous three or four tracks, that isn't enough. It has the verses, the pre-chorus, the chorus, the solos in the expected place – essentially, it's a nice bit of '80s 'Iron Maiden by numbers'. Even Dickinson has hinted as much when he has described the song in an interview at the time with *Classic Rock* magazine as 'A fairly conventional tuneful Maiden rocker comparable with a "Die With Your Boots On" type thing', which I couldn't have put better.

Apparently, the song was written about a bounty hunter, but was titled 'The Mercenary' as that was felt to be a better title than 'The Bounty Hunter'. It has been suggested that it could be inspired by the 1987 film *Predator*, owing to the reference to Diablo in the lyric, and lines which could easily relate to the movie, but none of the band have ever commented on that theory.

'Dream of Mirrors' (Gers, Harris)

Another Harris epic now to put us back on track. Written with the increasingly prolific Gers, this one comes in at just a shade under nine-and-a-half minutes, and it is worth every second. Lyrically, this is Harris looking at the subject of dreams – or more specifically, nightmares – to explore what he called 'the dark side of things ... people's thoughts and the suffering that may result from them, particularly at night'. So, another light-hearted, Steve Harris romp, then.

Actually, the lyric is very powerful, if indeed extremely dark, and Dickinson has described it as one of Steve's best. Speaking to *Classic Rock,* he called the chorus 'one of the best he's ever written', noting how heavy and weird he found the line 'I only dream in black and white' to be. He also, amusingly, stated 'Oh man, he's a tortured motherfucker, Steve is sometimes!', which I think is essentially a given – but it ha produced some great songs over the years for sure.

Musically this goes against type, as it actually comes in on a big heavy note for the first few lines, before settling down to a lengthy slow, quieter section, which is the opposite to the standard 'Maiden formula' if you like. The big opening seems to conjure the fear of the dreamer before he gets more reflective about what his dreams may mean. The chorus is, as Bruce correctly states, absolutely immense, and erupts from the quiet surroundings like a man awakening in panic. The quiet verse accompaniment begins again, driven by a subtle yet undeniable impetus from the rhythm section, while delightful little guitar curlicues are woven around it.

In fact, one of the key things to note about this album as a whole is just how much the three-guitar lineup has enhanced things, even if sometimes you may not notice unless you listen for it. Little harmonic licks and delicate touches of musical colour are all over the quieter sections, while there are more lead guitar fills and themes than ever in the big sections. Instrumental parts can have so much lead work going on, that at first you wonder whether the solo has started. The retaining of Janick for the third guitar may be one of the best decisions the band ever made.

When we get past the second chorus in this track, a frantic mid-section is hurled at us, with a punchy, tight series of lines all beginning 'Lost...', followed by the chorus repeated at double tempo. We're not done yet, however, as it's 'dive, dive, dive' into an instrumental whirlpool of slashing rhythm guitars and Janick's breathless solo. Back to the chorus, a short quiet coda, and we're done. Another epic in the can on what is proving a remarkable comeback album.

'The Fallen Angel' (Smith, Harris)

Another much shorter song, this fairly fast-paced track is nevertheless superior to 'The Mercenary'. Opening with a heavy harmony guitar intro which is straight from the Thin Lizzy manual (imagine 'Emerald' crossed with 'Warrior' and you're not far off) it follows that pre-chorus / chorus template so beloved by Maiden more than probably any other band, but both are catchy without being truly anthemic. Unusually, all three guitarists take a short solo in quick succession, beginning with Adrian Smith. Murray takes the honours with a dazzling display of focused brevity, while Gers has a different chordal backing to play over. Some nice lead guitar work comes in halfway through each chorus which, like the octave switch in 'Brave New World', prevents an attack of what we might call 'Angel and the Gambler syndrome'.

Lyrically this is Harris getting all heavy and biblical again (Smith wrote the basic music), although the meaning is unclear. Azazel is the fallen angel of the title, referred to in the opening line, but it also references the biblical story of the goat symbolically carrying the sins of the Hebrews being cast out and sent to him (Azazel is often translated as 'goat of departure', or 'escape goat', leading to the term scapegoat). It would appear that what Harris has done here is to take the Azazel story as a jumping-off point and apply his own dark vision to it. In fact, Dickinson commented that he seemed to be having 'a lot of dark patches' at the time, and expressed the hope that if released as a single it would not cause people to hurl themselves from windows in despair. He needn't have worried; it wasn't chosen for single release.

'Nomad' (Murray, Harris)

This sprawling, expansive nine-minute behemoth is not only quite different to anything else on the album – and indeed most of Maiden's catalogue – but it is also unquestionably one of their best ensemble pieces ever. Lyrically, the track is fairly simple, with no hidden obscure meanings or tantalising clues. It is simply a tribute to, and evocation of, the Bedouin: the mysterious desert-dwellers of the title. That simplicity works, however, as this desert image gives the inspiration to the whole sound of the piece, and it can carry the listener away in his or her imagination like few other Maiden pieces.

No quiet introductions or anything here, as the band just slam right in with a slow, rolling Arabic-sounding riff in the proud tradition of 'Kashmir', 'Stargazer' or 'Perfect Strangers'. The verses are constant throughout, but the chorus changes mid-song. The first chorus is repeated twice, but from the third chorus on it changes musically to a slower and grander melody, though each line still begins with 'Nomad...'

Where the track really takes off and receives many of its plaudits, however, is in the instrumental section beginning just after the four-and-a-half-minute mark and lasting for over three minutes. The sound drops to a quieter interlude bringing to mind night-time in the desert, with the tents pitched and the men relaxing, but after a minute or so it builds into a riff which can only be described as the image of a vast caravan of camels and men crossing the horizon against a setting Sun. The guitars spiral around the crushing, relentless riffing until, as we pass the seven-minute mark, the listener is likely to be transfixed. Just before eight minutes, in comes Bruce again for another big verse and chorus, and it's gone. There are solos in the song – three of them, a verse before the instrumental section, by Smith, Gers then Murray, but in this case, they are far from the instrumental focus, and the track would have worked without them, good as they are. It has been commented that the true spiritual home of this song would have been the *Powerslave* album, and that is a powerful argument indeed.

The music bears a distinct inspiration from a song by Beckett (remember the cover that Maiden did as a B-side) called 'Life's Shadow', but the way it is fed through the Maiden mincer renders it a whole different beast. Harris was, of course, a big fan of this obscure band, and after the gesture of covering one of their tracks, few would carp about plagiarism of a band whose name Maiden have almost single-handedly kept alive. Astonishingly, this magnificent track has never been played live – scandalous, really, as it would surely have made an incredible stage number. Perhaps the band tried it but couldn't do it justice, in a similar way to Rainbow with 'Gates of Babylon'; who knows. That lack of live performance has led it to be overlooked, which is a shame.

Bruce Dickinson referred to the song as 'Carry On Follow That Camel' which is very amusing, but certainly rather misleading!

'Out of the Silent Planet' (Gers, Dickinson, Harris)

The title of this song, of course, comes from a book of the same name by CS Lewis, in which Earth is the 'Silent Planet' because it will not respond to any efforts at communication. The lyrics do not have a direct connection to this book, however, with Dickinson always claiming he had a different sci-fi inspiration in mind. Many people have attributed different meanings to this song, with such things as nuclear holocaust, ecological disaster, war and the politics of hate and bigotry all jostling for elbow room. Bruce's claim is simpler, however: according to him, the direct inspiration was the 1956 film *Forbidden Planet*, claiming it was a little like a sci-fi 'Run to the Hills' with aliens who have destroyed their world leaving their silent planet and coming to ours. It may lack some of the poetry of the more esoteric interpretations, but it does fit in a literal way – and since he wrote the words, he should know.

Released as the second single, it seems an odd choice for that as, while catchy, it lacks the real 'ear-worm' quality of something like 'Brave New World'. It's also peculiar that, as a single, it was only played live a handful of times. It reached Number 20 in the UK charts. Musically, it has several mood changes, with (again) a quiet intro and first chorus. Again, there are two different choruses, with the really catchy one simply repeating 'Out of the silent planet, out of the silent planet we are', with a guitar playing the vocal melody as a nice added touch. The music reached a familiar gallop, but when the solo (by Gers alone) comes in, the backing had slowed to a grinding, almost atonal riff, with the squealing, tortured solo conjuring to these ears the actual invasion taking place. It may not be the greatest song on the album, but it's a good one, and it has a lot of competition on this record.

'The Thin Line Between Love and Hate' (Murray, Harris)

This is a rather strange track in a couple of ways. It is eight-and-a-half minutes long, and as the album closer as well, one might expect a deep, multi-faceted epic, but this delivers none of that. Not to say that is a bad song, but it is a straightforward, heavy, bludgeoning track for most of its duration, being extended by a quite lengthy instrumental section – which is brilliant in itself but does not offer much in the way of light and shade, except for a relatively brief section at around five-and-a-half minutes, returning at the very end. The title, as sung by Dickinson a couple of times in these quiet parts, sounds most un-Maiden-like. He said at the time that the track reminded him 'of a UFO song in a way', and while I can't quite see that for the most part, that line does sound a little like a vocal melody Phil Mogg might come up with. Nicko can be heard at the very end, complaining that he missed the end of the song, which he hadn't.

What the song most definitely is, above all else, is an absolute guitar tour-de-force, especially for Dave Murray who is front and centre in all of the main solos. Essentially, after five minutes or so it becomes Dave's Guitar Workshop, and the rather forgettable vocal part of the song is forgiven. In the end, a decent ending to an album which is not only a great comeback of sorts but on its own terms sits right towards the very top of the Maiden pantheon. With two decades having elapsed since the first album, this was extraordinary stuff by any standards.

There are no related songs, as the single releases from the album all used live versions of existing tracks as B-sides

Dance of Death

Personnel:
Bruce Dickinson: vocals
Dave Murray: guitars
Janick Gers: guitars
Adrian Smith: guitars
Steve Harris: bass guitar, keyboards
Nicko McBrain: drums
Record Label: EMI (UK), Columbia (US)
Recorded: Jan-Feb 2003, produced by Kevin Shirley and Steve Harris
Release date: 8 September 2003
Highest chart places: UK: 7, USA: 39
Running time: 67:57

First confirmed to the world in November 2002, as the band announced some
European dates for the following June as part of their 'Give Me Ed 'Til I'm
Dead' tour, which preceded the release of the album, *Dance of Death* was
recorded very quickly. The band went into the studio with Kevin Shirley in
January, and by 5 February it was announced that the recording was complete.
However, the mixing was not done until April, with the release date eventually
announced in June to be 8 September – Japan was seemingly too impatient, as
they got the jump on the rest of the world by releasing on 2 September. This
is a somewhat odd delay following the recording, but it was almost certainly
done to tie in with the gap between the two tours – the 'Dance of Death World
Tour' itself commenced in October and ran through to the following February.
Consisting of only 53 shows, while still lengthy it was a respite from some of
their gruelling schedules in the past.

The recording of the album continued the decision taken with *Brave New
World* to stay away from Harris's barn and was undertaken at SARM West
Studios, Notting Hill, London, which had previously been Island Studios,
and Basing Street Studios (SARM stands for Sound and Recording Mobiles).
A facility with some pedigree, the studio had firmly established its rock
credentials in 1970 when both *Led Zeppelin IV* and Jethro Tull's *Aqualung*
were recorded there.

Album Cover:

Ah, now we hit some controversy. As bad as the reaction to the *X Factor* cover
had been, this was worse. When the band unveiled the absurd collage of odd
characters around a Reaper Eddie, some people assumed it was a joke to
avoid the real cover being leaked. The band had engaged digital artist David
Patchett to do the cover, but you won't find his name in the credits, as I will
come to shortly. Patchett produced a first draft which consisted simply of
Eddie and some hooded monks in the background, some of which can still
be seen behind the mask-wearing freakshow on the finished cover. It is at this

point that stories diverge. It has been claimed that Rod Smallwood thought that it looked empty, and he gave it to someone from the band's website to add the extra characters, which Patchett then tried to improve but without much success. Alternatively, the official band explanation was that these CGI foreground characters were indeed Patchett's work, but that he only presented the design as a rough, which was chosen to be released as it was. What is certain is that Patchett was so unhappy with the final result that he asked for his name to be removed from the credits to avoid embarrassment.

To be honest, it's easy to understand his frustration. The final design looks amateurish in the extreme, with glaring issues throughout, but a couple of things stand out spectacularly. The woman in the right foreground has a neck which is physically impossible unless she was a bizarre hybrid of man and giraffe, while a white wolf next to Eddie has a baby riding on its back which is so misplaced that it doesn't even make contact with the animal. Add that to the ridiculous expression on this would-be noble beast's face, and Patchett clearly had the right idea. The glory days of Derek Riggs seemed long ago, and Bruce Dickinson later described the cover himself as 'embarrassing'.

The back cover, with the band looking rather bored on and around a red settee, also fails to get the pulses racing, though at least the booklet design is excellent this time out, with some intriguing photos featuring a blurred, 'ghostly' woman. Small victories, I suppose.

'Wildest Dreams' (Smith, Harris)

A fairly straightforward fast Maiden album opener, this song was, in fact, the only one the band played on the 'Give Me Ed 'Til I'm Dead' dates before the album release. The lyric is simple, just a positive message to take hold of your life and make things happen for yourself rather than have any past regrets. The same thing was done in 'Wasted Years', but rather better.

'Wildest Dreams' isn't bad; in fact, it's rather good for what it is. It's just that its only real purpose seems to be an upbeat album opener that people can punch the air and sing along to at gigs – the chorus is certainly good for that. Adrian Smith's solo is also strong, but there isn't much real substance here. You feel that Maiden could churn these songs out by the bucketload if they wanted to. It was a single as well, which is a pretty obvious choice, and it did its job, reaching Number Six in the UK charts. The voice heard counting in at the beginning is, of course, Nicko.

A word of advice, however – feel free to enjoy 'Wildest Dreams' as the uncomplicated fun it is, but don't be tempted to watch the official video for the song, as it is appalling. A computer-generated short with hopeless band likenesses, it features the six band members in sub-*Mario Kart* racing sequences, before they end up meeting Eddie, in his worst incarnation ever. A huge figure in a top hat and brandishing a whip, he is trying to keep control over a horde of tiny masked minions who are headbanging and playing air guitar. Yes, you read that correctly. They are headbanging and playing air guitar.

The Ancient Mariner is turning in his watery grave. But wait, there's more, as these tiny speeding Maiden Monkees drive into Eddie's mouth and down his throat in a sequence which practically screams to be made into a video game. The single sleeve has a screenshot from the video as its design. That's horrible as well.

'Rainmaker' (Murray, Harris, Dickinson)

Another short song, with the lyric again being quite a simple one – certainly by Dickinson standards (he wrote the lyric while Dave Murray wrote most of the music and Harris pitched in with a few melodies). The desert is used as an allegory for our lives, with the way a desert can bloom quickly if subjected to rainfall equating to how our own happiness, or 'rain', can change our lives just as quickly. It's a better song than 'Wildest Dreams', though it does suffer a little from over-repetition of the chorus, and Dave Murray's solo is exceptionally good, though, with the song coming in at under four minutes it should really have been longer and more developed. It's very good, if not quite great.

Released as the second single, hitting Number 13 in the UK, this again had an official video, although it was not all that widely shown. It bears comparison to the classic 1980s Maiden videos, with a live performance cut with footage of a motley collection of characters, some clearly based on the album cover. As the rain bursts out of some of these characters as they hover over the stage, the band get more and more drenched until they are playing in a flood. The video is in black and white, which was presumably for artistic effect, but just ends up rather dull. The cover art for the single is once again a still from the video – although coloured at least – which displays a shocking lack of imagination or indeed care as regards the single designs, perhaps because downloads were already becoming more common than even CD singles? It's a shame, though.

'No More Lies' (Harris)

Three songs in, and we have the first real classic on the album. In fact, this song, while an immediate one musically and a fan favourite, is probably one of the most misunderstood songs in the Maiden catalogue, with casual listeners focusing, understandably, on the oft-repeated title phrase and simply taking the subject of not wanting to be lied to any more, as the thrust of the song. As is so often the case with Harris songs (note that this is his only solo writing credit on the album), there is much more going on. The central character in the song is a man who has reached the end of his life, without any regrets and is musing over the possibility of being reincarnated, or else going on to an afterlife, if there is one. Whatever the truth, he will know it soon, as will all of his fellow 'end of lifers', who he sees as unknowingly sitting at a table, talking and drinking wine. There will be 'no more lies', as all of the answers to life and death will be revealed.

Harris himself has stated that the Last Supper was an influence on the song, which would feed into the friends at his table drinking wine, so an interpretation might be that the narrator of the song is, in fact, Jesus Christ, and the 'being back again' is the Second Coming. All very thought-provoking stuff for a song with a title as simple as 'No More Lies', and that phrase is repeated again and again. Does anyone else do this sort of juxtaposition of the simple and the deep quite like Maiden?

Musically this is right on the money. A beautiful quiet intro, taking in the first verses, takes up the first two-and-a-half minutes of the song, before the almost military pounding of the drums in the chorus ushers in the band almost as if they crashed in through a window on a rope! Unlike the previous two songs, this one is fast but also crunchingly, unstoppably powerful, which is best realised in the chorus where midway through, the staccato rhythm is released into a rampaging riff. Once again, the 'chorus of two halves' is a quite brilliant effect and one at which the band are becoming the masters. All three axemen get in on the act, with the solos being Murray, Smith, Gers in quick succession, but again it is the interweaving of the guitars which is the true hero here, from the delicate picking of the intro to the instrumental with its shades of Wishbone Ash again (there are real echoes of their classic 'Throw Down the Sword' in here, to great effect). A great song, and a live classic.

'Montségur' (Gers, Harris, Dickinson)

By some way the heaviest song on the album, this one is almost six minutes of bludgeoning riffery, with no letup. In a way, the musical structure of the song is at odds with the lyrics, which are another fascinating Maiden history lesson. Bruce Dickinson had become fascinated by the story of the Cathars when he visited the former citadel of Montségur in what is now Southern France and was inspired to write this song, with Gers (mostly) providing the music.

The Cathars were a Medieval Christian sect from the 13th Century, whose beliefs, including that of a dual deity with a merciful God ruling heaven and an evil Satan ruling the physical world, were denounced as heresy by the mainstream Church of the time. To cut a long story short, a ten-month siege of the Cathar stronghold of Montségur – which at that time was in a region between France and Spain yet controlled by neither – resulted in their defeat, and the voluntary martyrdom at the stake of their leaders, the 'Perfects'. It is claimed, though dubiously, that the Knights Templar also got involved and rode to the Cathars' aid. Dickinson conveys this superbly in his lyric, which calls to mind the glory days of historical epics like 'Alexander the Great' and the like.

Musically things are a little too one-dimensional, with some light and shade probably fitting the lyrical content more, but the real let-down of this song is the 'post-chorus' verse which begins 'As we kill them all'. From the dark, heavy verses and main chorus, this part, with a chirpy sounding guitar following the vocal melody, sounds so upbeat and 'singalong' that it is more 'Sesame Street' than 'Acacia Avenue'. It doesn't provide any contrast as it remains heavy, but it still manages to kill the dramatic mood. Janick takes the guitar solo duty here and does so well, but the song has never been played live to my knowledge.

Probably wisely. It's a little bit of a missed opportunity with a great lyric.

'Dance of Death' (Gers, Harris)

This epic and decidedly cinematic tale of demonic goings-on deep in the Florida Everglades is clearly intended as the centrepiece of the album (along with 'Paschendale', which we'll get to shortly). In fact, Janick Gers had the original idea for the song's concept after seeing the 1957 Ingmar Bergman film *The Seventh Seal* (you know, the one where the knight plays chess with the devil for his soul). He loved the film, and in particular the final scene – filmed by Bergman without the cast knowing about it – which pans out to reveal people dancing to music which was the 'dance of death'. In the end, after it had been filtered through the surreal mind of Steve Harris, the plot had changed to a rather more straightforward horror tale with the protagonist being waylaid by a gang of undead on an away-day from hell. He ends up dancing with them before 'a skirmish' mysteriously breaks out and he gets away. In truth, it isn't really one of Harris's best lyrics – the story is rather 'Spinal Tap', to say the least, while his old problem of putting an irregular number of syllables into lines is back with a vengeance. Plus, he uses the words 'and I danced and I pranced', which really isn't a good idea. Still, it's fun in a 'B-movie horror' sort of way.

Musically it's a bit uneven, with some great parts, but also some clumsy bits over its near nine-minute duration. It begins with a long, slow-building intro over the first three minutes or so, as the scene is set, with drums and guitars gradually entering – it's a refreshing change from 'right, a minute of quiet guitars then we throw the whole lot in', but it could have been smoother. The moment when everything is indeed thrown in is certainly an awkward transition, but it's accompanied by a nice Celtic sort of jig, which conjures up the dancing, but by the same token sounds a little bit too cheery in a 'round-the-maypole' sort of way. Things pick up significantly when the guitar solos come in, however, with Smith and Gers getting sixteen bars apiece, while Murray in the middle of the two gets only eight, with a little instrumental part showing off the unison guitars before Gers takes flight. Smith, in particular, is immense here. The vocals come back, with a final 'chorus'-like part, which is sung far too quickly and sounds a bit like Dickinson is doing a tongue-twister, before the quiet bit is back, our hero maintains he will dance no more until he dances with the dead again, and we're done.

Clearly, from the verse after the instrumental part, it is clear that those who participate in the dance of the dead are normally on their way to the afterlife with the motley crew of demons, but that he has miraculously cheated death as he escaped. As I said, it's an entertaining song, and fun to listen to, but I can't put it right into the upper echelon of Maiden epics.

'Gates of Tomorrow' (Gers, Harris, Dickinson)

If it was a slightly contentious opinion not to consider the previous track a classic, here it is almost a consensus among fans – this one has 'filler' written all over it, in letters ten feet high. In luminous paint. The lyric is okay, in a typically enigmatic Dickinson way, with the first part appearing to be a being sitting in judgement, and the pre-chorus and chorus sections which follow hint at taking the responsibility for one's own fate, and refusing to follow the path which is written for you. So far, so good.

Musically, however, this sounds like a throwaway which would have been shipped off to a B-side in the vinyl days when albums were shorter affairs. After an overlong intro which could be mistaken for 'Lord of the Flies' in a police line-up, all throbbing, ominous guitar, the band crash in with a clumsy thrash, devoid of any of the usual Maiden subtlety which is normally there even in the heaviest moments. There is no guitar interplay or nimble bass work here, just 'heads down and see you at the finish'. Worst of all are the two guitar solos, one after another, both delivered by Gers, which must rank as his worst Maiden work, sounding for all the world as if it is a mere run-through, in which he is trying to cram in as many notes as possible with no structure or feeling. On to the next track, because there really is nothing to see here.

'New Frontier' (McBrain, Smith, Dickinson)
Well, it only took 30 years – Nicko McBrain gets a songwriting credit! And it's not as if he just had a token involvement either, as this song was very much his 'baby' from the start, particularly regarding the lyrics, which are very personal to his beliefs. Since 1999, McBrain has been a born-again Christian, and one of the things he feels very strongly about is the idea of cloning, as he believes that as only God can give a man a soul, so only God can create life. This song is very much about that particular moral and ethical standpoint and has been the subject of much disapproval, especially among the scientific community, who understandably take it as a kind of attack on their moral compass. Leaving that aside, the lyrics are reasonably well written, and are quite acceptable.

Musically, while it is a fairly standard Maiden galloper, melodically the song is rather good, with the chorus, in particular, being excellent, and the band appear to be relishing the switchblade riffing that powers the verses along, as they sound positively energised. Smith and Murray take the solos here, and they are both quite superb. Some parts of the song, particularly the riffing going into the instrumental section, have a bit of a feel of the Di'Anno albums, but with Bruce in full flight as well, we get the best of both worlds.

According to the drummer, he wrote the melody and demoed it to the guys on bass, then enlisting Adrian Smith to finish it off with him – the part played by the also-credited Dickinson remains unclear. It's all essentially Nicko's foundations, though and he deserves much credit. He hasn't repeated the feat as yet, unfortunately.

'Paschendale' (Smith, Harris)
Here is the real epic centrepiece of the album, with this graphically moving

account of the Battle of Paschendale, the Third Battle of Ypres. Named after the French village nearby (actually spelt Passchendaele), the conflict involved exhausted troops who had spent weeks on end in deep mud and was among the worst horrors of the First World War. It is brought to vivid, unflinching life here through Steve Harris's superb lyrics.

Unusually, the music for the song was by Adrian Smith. By his own admission, he was mainly known for shorter, simpler Maiden songs, and this was his first crack at a 'proper Maiden epic', as he called it. We can safely say he passed the audition, as this is a masterpiece. Beginning with Nicko's eerie tapping beat, reminiscent of a Morse Code signal, and a plaintive guitar figure, the song alternates between quiet, pleading moments and huge bursts of crushing metal, like shells bursting all around. Things get big and consistently heavy as Bruce starts weaving the tale of a young man in the trench, simply waiting for what will be his inevitable death, and his colleagues being slaughtered around him. The music weaves between different riffs and tempos but always keeps up that intensity which gives the listener a claustrophobic feeling of being in the trenches amid the chaos and hell. Finally, the men go 'over the top' to be mown down, and after the line 'Rush of blood and over we go' Murray, and then Smith, take a couple of excellent solos over yet another heavy instrumental backing. One more verse ending 'And so we die at Paschendale' and it's Janick's turn to shine, completing a trio of top-class solos.

The protagonist gets, inevitably, taken down in a hail of gunfire, finishing with the lonely 'I choke a cry but no-one hears, feel the blood go down my throat', and it's time for a big, climactic chorus of 'Home, far away from the war', followed by a quiet ending dying out with 'Friend and foe will meet again, those who died at Paschendale'. This is not just great metal, not just great lyric writing – this is great music and great art. And this is the kind of thing which Iron Maiden do better than anyone else. It is a magnificent tribute to those who fell in the war, and food for thought in terms of not letting anything like it happen again.

'Face in the Sand' (Smith, Harris, Dickinson)
This is another great song, with Dickinson exploring the idea of a catastrophe striking the world, while the stupefied masses simply watch the end unfold on TV. Opening with a quiet intro, bearing more than a passing resemblance to 'Dance of Death', the music slowly builds in a remorseless fashion until the band come in around the 90-second mark, keeping the same relentless grind as the opening. The vocals don't come until about two minutes, which is almost a third of the way through the song, but we don't miss them as the propulsive bass and drums and slashing chords from the guitars keep us fully engaged. The instrumental section, when it comes, is different from the rest of the song but contains a magnificent solo from Smith alone.

This one simply never lets up, and with its strong chorus factored into proceedings is without doubt one of the best songs on the album. It had been needing a bit of a boost after a slight sag before 'Paschendale', and my word was it getting it.

Unfortunately, this song has never been played live, mainly because Nicko McBrain resisted it. The first Maiden song ever on which he used a double bass drum pedal, he described it as one of the most demanding songs he's had to play, and requested not to have to do it on a nightly basis!

'Age of Innocence' (Murray, Harris)

Harris gets a bit political again here, and polarises the listeners once again, in this rant against the perceived soft justice and lax attitudes to crime by the forces of law in modern Britain. He laments the inability of ordinary people to protect themselves and their families from attack for fear of being themselves punished as 'vigilantes' and looks back at the 'age of innocence' of his youth, which is fading 'like an old dream'. It's hard to disagree with much of what he says, or with the heartfelt belief he himself has in it, but this sort of thing is always going to be a contentious subject. The case of farmer Tony Martin, imprisoned for shooting an intruder in his home, certainly seems to be a factor here, with the words 'You can't protect yourselves even in your own home, for fear of vigilante cries'. This was a case which showed that there could never be a black-and-white consensus about this kind of thing. Whatever your own feelings about the song, or mine, it is certain that others will be as vehement about it the other way.

Musically, it is a cracker. One of Murray's occasional songs, as far as the music goes, it is hard-hitting with the lyrics spat out by Dickinson in a voice filled with righteous vitriol. There is a very strong chorus as well, a soaring melody which contrasts with the bruising verses perfectly. Murray himself plays all the guitar solos here; one in the lovely quiet opening, and two more standard ones during the main body of the song.

Steve Harris claimed at the time that the song was 'not political, Maiden don't do that', which is an astonishing claim given the subjects such as the Falklands, the Iraqi war and others in recent times. Sorry Steve, with lines like 'all the politicians with their hollow promises', 'a life of petty crime gets punished with a holiday', 'they know the laws are soft, conviction chances low' and, finally, the best of all in 'so now the criminals they laugh right in our face, judicial system lets them do it, a disgrace', you simply can't claim 'not political'. As I said, it may well be a very good point, but it is as political as the day is long!

'Journeyman' (Smith, Harris, Dickinson)

The first all-acoustic track of Maiden's career closes the album, and it undoubtedly is a beautiful song. The lyrics by Dickinson refer, according to the singer himself, to the choices we have in life, and whether we can choose to live a safe existence or a mad and glorious life is up to us. There is more to the lyric, though – the 'shadows made with our hands' appear to represent the fact that everything we do is temporary, and the talk of turning to the light seems to allude

113

to some sort of moral or religious choice. Why have we 'cheated death' but he has also 'cheated us'? And what is the dream, and its connection to Winter?

Of course, one of the great things about Bruce's lyrics, generally more so than the more literal Harris, are the clues he leaves to fire the listener's imagination. If you listen carefully during the instrumental section (no solos here, guys!), you can hear the singer whispering what seems to be the second verse, which he then reprises. This again is something which makes one wonder about the significance it may have.

Initially, the chorus, which sparked the song, was intended to become a grand anthemic track, but this was bravely discarded in favour of this charming and soothing arrangement, and it is a great album closer. They even played it during the encore of the accompanying tour, in fully acoustic mode, to respectful attention from the audiences. Of course, the full electric version was released separately, as we shall see...

Related songs:
'Pass the Jam' (Dickinson, Gers, Harris, McBrain, Murray, Smith)
After a couple of albums where the related B-sides were all live versions of existing songs, we now get a new title again. Don't get excited though, we aren't lucky. This addition to the 'Wildest Dreams' single is an example of that beast which tends to excite bands far more than any listeners: the jam. And this is no exception to that rule, as it goes on for an interminable eight-and-a-half minutes. The band settle into a nice enough groove which takes about two minutes to go from 'that's not bad' to 'oh God, please make it stop', while Dickinson ad-libs words which might have been funny if you were there. Maybe. Or maybe not. Listening to the track, the time when mentally pleading for the end of this torture takes over is around four minutes, at which time the realisation hits that they're only halfway through. Listen to it if you like, it will be a one-off experience.

Transcriptions of the lyrics have often had the first of the four lines about Julius Caesar and Brutus as 'Caesar had some jam with tea', but this is incorrect. Any English schoolboy of a certain age will remember the cod-Latin 'poem' 'Caesar adsum jam forte / Brutus adarat / Caesar sic in omnibus / Brutus sic inat' (say it out loud) – and it is that which Bruce is referencing with the line being 'for tea'. The 'joke poem' is referred to in the classic Nigel Molesworth books by Geoffrey Willans and Ronald Searle, which Ian Gillan also referred to in the song title 'Any Fule Kno That'. There you go, something moderately worth talking about as regards this ghastly recording exercise!

The single was rounded off by an 'orchestral' version of 'Blood Brothers', which is essentially a bit of synthesizer shoved onto the original and is utterly worthless.

'More Tea Vicar' (Dickinson, Gers, Harris, McBrain, Murray, Smith)
What's that you hear? Yes, it's the poor completists who bought the 'Rainmaker' single for this track wailing and gnashing their teeth. Yup, it's another jam. And guess what – it's worse than 'Pass the Jam'! Mind you, it's four minutes

shorter. The band don't make any effort to produce anything worthwhile, and the 'lyric' consists mainly of Dickinson shouting the title in a 'posh' voice. The phrase is an English thing, said when someone does something offensive, like a particularly impressive fart. There's also a repeated a joke about said vicar 'fiddling with his organ'. It's hardly Oscar Wilde, let's put it that way. He also manages to make the joke about being 'uncouth' as 'without couth', only 30 years after Alice Cooper did it in 'Department of Youth'. Towards the end, there is a mildly entertaining Bee Gees impression, but it's far too little too late. There may be a double meaning with the title having the initials MTV, but nobody particularly cared. Stop doing this guys – your B-sides used to be great.

The single also contains another 'orchestral version', this time of 'Dance of Death'. To be fair, it has more differences than the 'Blood Brothers' one did, so it may be found to be mildly entertaining, but I couldn't in all conscience advise anyone to waste ten minutes finding out.

'Journeyman (Electric Version)' (Smith, Harris, Dickinson)

This is from the 'No More Lies' EP (or *Dance of Death Souvenir EP* if you prefer), which was a rather disposable little box containing a CD, a thin booklet and a hopeless 'souvenir wristband', presumably for all those one-armed Maiden fans out there. Or maybe you were supposed to buy two copies? Anyhow, once you get past 'No More Lies' and another useless 'orchestral version' – this time smearing a coating of Vaseline all over 'Paschendale', to detrimental effect – you reach the real meat of the release: this original electric version of 'Journeyman' which was initially intended for the album. It's pretty good and certainly interesting to hear, but overall it probably reinforces the decision to use the far more subtle acoustic version. The whispering by Dickinson in the instrumental section is louder here, incidentally.

If you let the disc play on after this, you get one of those 'hilarious' – read 'utterly infuriating' – 'hidden tracks' which were all the rage for a while, whereby you have to sit through a period of silence, which in this case is six minutes long, before something you knew full well was there, suddenly pipes up. In this case, it's 'Days of Innocence ... How Old?' This is essentially a joke rendition of 'Age of Innocence' with Nicko singing and getting the words wrong, mumbling to himself, losing where he's up to, and delivering it all with a sort of old-fashioned 'cockney policeman' voice (think "Ello Ello Ello, wot's been goin' on 'ere then?', sort of thing). It should be terrible, and for much of the time it is, but there are funny moments and the point where he 'sings' along with Dave Murray's solo, going 'Dee dee wa wa wah wankadidy dah da' has to be heard at least once. Still these are slim pickings for the 'Souvenir EP' released as a 'thank you to the fans' though, it must be said.

Oh yes, there's one more addition. A video for 'No More Lies' which purports to be a live performance, but actually syncs live footage to the studio track and tries to conceal it by dubbing in crowd noise. So ironically, it lies to the listener. We should probably move on.

A Matter of Life and Death

Personnel:
Bruce Dickinson: vocals
Dave Murray: guitars
Janick Gers: guitars
Adrian Smith: guitars
Steve Harris: bass guitar, keyboards
Nicko McBrain: drums
Record Label: EMI (UK), Sanctuary (US)
Recorded: March-May 2006, produced by Kevin Shirley and Steve Harris
Release date: 28 August 2006
Highest chart places: UK: 4, USA: 9
Running time: 71:53

After the *Dance of Death* world tour, the band embarked on a short 45-date Summer tour in 2005 called the 'Eddie Rips Up the World Tour', which was a nostalgic exercise (and treat for younger or newer fans) featuring songs only from the first four albums. Following that, and a deserved break, at the end of 2005, they started writing material for the next album. Following a Christmas hiatus, the songs were completed in early 2006, and in March the band returned to SARM West studios to commence recording of *A Matter of Life and Death*. To give the album a more 'live', raw sound, Steve Harris, along with co-producer Kevin Shirley, elected not to master the album, so that no EQ or smoothing of any kind would be applied. The resulting sound is certainly very good and suits the material which, while not a concept album *per se*, has a constant thread running through it concerning war, destruction, death and general hopelessness for humanity. Well, nobody was expecting a 'Nicko Mix' anyway!

On the resulting tour, the band took one of their most contentious decisions ever, which saw them play the entire album from start to finish, followed by just five older songs – 'Fear of the Dark', 'Iron Maiden', and an encore of '2 Minutes to Midnight', 'The Evil That Men Do' and 'Hallowed Be Thy Name'. This caused a heated debate among fans, with a great many complaints about the decision, which certainly was a big chunk for anyone not yet familiar with the album. The band defended themselves by saying they were still a vital force and that this showed it, and fans who agreed with them turned on others by claiming they just wanted to hear 'The Trooper' and 'Run to the Hills' again. In fact, that criticism was somewhat unjustified, as the album is a long one, similar to a vinyl double, and the show was only around two hours. Many claimed there should have been a longer show with no support, and it is hard to disagree with this. Personally, having attended the tour, I emphatically did not want those old songs yet again. Rather, I wanted such post-reunion material as 'Brave New World', 'Blood Brothers' or 'Paschendale', none of which had managed to get stale in the least by that time. In any case, the lesson seemed to have been learned and, when touring the next album, only five songs from its ten would be played live.

Album Cover:
There was still no room for a Riggs Return, as this time out the cover art is by noted comic book artist Tim Bradstreet. Depicting Eddie in a defiant pose atop a tank, with five undead soldiers in front, it was undoubtedly better received than the *Dance of Death* cover but still polarised the fanbase. While many expressed their dislike for it, owing to its lesser depiction of Eddie, who is in the background and far less recognisable than usual, others declared that to be a good thing. This was because the cover reflected the album's themes more accurately rather than being just another 'let's see what we can make Eddie into this time' exercise. As with most things of this divisive ilk, the truth can be seen as somewhere in between. Certainly, there have been times when the 'having to show Eddie' thing has perhaps hampered a cover (*The X Factor* and *No Prayer for the Dying* as two candidates), but the final design lacks something in the way of immediate impact. Bradstreet was an avowed Maiden fan and declared the chance to do the artwork as 'one of my wildest dreams', which may or may not have been a deliberate pun! The back cover was originally to have been another Bradstreet illustration depicting Eddie, but for some reason, the band elected to go with the rather drab and dull 'crossed rifles' image on the tank in close up. It has been suggested that Eddie and the five zombie soldiers could represent the six members of Maiden, but there has never been any official encouragement of that story. Nevertheless, you can have fun deciding who would be who: for my money, Harris would be Eddie, in command and carrying his rifle like the bass; Dickinson on the right out in front; Nicko as the one front left, simply because somehow it manages to look like him, undead or not; Smith would be on the tank, smoking; and finally, of the other two, Murray would be the one rear left, in the sense of always being there without ever saying that much.

'Different World' (Smith, Harris)
Another fairly typical Maiden album-opener, this one is sort of a more thoughtful take on 'Wildest Dreams' in a way, with the message seeming to be that nothing should be taken as an absolute fact in this world, as everybody sees it a different way. It ties into the anti-war theme to an extent, as one could extrapolate this to show the futility of trying to impose one's will or beliefs on others when everybody sees the world differently. The lyric could also be seen to express the philosophy of solipsism, by which one's own perception of the world is the only true one. For instance, what one man sees as the colour red, and names as red, may be seen as blue by someone else, but would still be red in his or her own world. Whatever the meaning, it's a beautifully melodic and very memorable chorus, backed up by some powerful riffing and a fine Adrian Smith solo.

The song has been described as something of a tip of the hat to Thin Lizzy – an influence on the band for sure – and while not explicit, this can certainly be heard in some of the Phil Lynott-type phrasings in the chorus and, most directly, at the beginning of the instrumental section just before Smith begins soloing. There was an official video for the single release (Number Three in the UK charts, perhaps surprisingly), which is a computer-animated load of old tosh, to be honest. The sub-Playstation graphics depict an absurd plot with Dickinson – for no apparent reason – singing in a futuristic drone factory sorting test tubes. Seeing one tube with liquid of a different purple colour, he stops singing, whips out a moulded carry case which he happens to have, and makes good his escape with the tube, pursued by enraged drones. Via a walkway, a zeppelin, a ride with a flying drone and some good old fast footwork, he heads for a clairvoyant who shows him a new vision, in which more flying drones drop eggs into the sea, as one does of course, and they sprout new greenery before a young version of our hero Bruce as a boy appears, opens the case and hurls the tube at the screen, smashing it. Naturally, this leads to a yet more preposterous vision in which a giant Eddie rampages around destroying entire cities like a witless Heavy Metal Godzilla before we zoom out to see the whole world held in the hand of another Eddie. 'Deep and Meaningless', I believe the phrase is. Still, there is the odd glimpse of the band playing on screens within the video, which are clips taken from yet another video they released for it. Confused? Don't be, it's not worth it. Just listen to the song.

'These Colours Don't Run' (Smith, Harris, Dickinson)

This is another Maiden war song, comparable with the likes of 'Paschendale', 'Afraid to Shoot Strangers' and 'The Trooper', but with another slightly different lyrical perspective. The song looks at the different reasons people have for joining the Armed Forces to go and fight, be it glory, passion, money, whatever the driving force may be, once you're in the field of combat it's all the same. The line 'these colours don't run' is, of course, a pun on colours on fabric running into one another when washed, and has been used for a long time in the sense of no cowardice when representing one's flag or regiment. Dickinson has said that all soldiers are essentially heroes in the final analysis, whoever they may be fighting for, but that is a topic which has been endlessly debated, sometimes hotly, on Iron Maiden message boards the length and breadth of the Internet. Most believe that the song is making a more subtle point about the futility of fighting rather than merely praising the glory and courage of the soldiers in battle, with some even claiming the song is as ironically rabble-rousing as 'Born in the USA', but in the final analysis we can't second guess Bruce on this one.

Musically, it's a good song. It isn't a great one. There are great parts, certainly, but the way they fit together is at times awkward, and they feel a little bolted together, such as going into the chorus and transitioning back out again. The quiet intro (a Maiden trademark by now) is very nice, but again, the abrupt lurch into the full band is jarring. Murray produces a nice solo, with the one following by Smith slightly less effective, but overall it's a decent effort. Interestingly, some time before the album was recorded, during the infamous spat between Bruce and Sharon Osbourne, when the band were playing with Ozzy and she placed people at the front to throw eggs at Bruce as he waved the British flag, he uttered the exact phrase 'These colours don't run' in defiance. It could be that this incident planted the seed for the song.

'Brighter Than a Thousand Suns' (Smith, Harris, Dickinson)

A dramatic shift in lyrical emphasis for this one – though still loosely within the 'war' concept – as this brilliant lyric laments the dawn of the nuclear age, and the growth of the escalating 'balance of terror'. This sought to keep the equilibrium via the so-called 'Mutually Assured Destruction' scenario but has found itself on an ever more unstable fulcrum as more and more countries, some with less than stable political situations, have joined the race to stockpile.

The song title, of course, comes from the description of an atom bomb detonation's brightness, but the song is full of superlative wordplay and neat allusions. The description of the nuclear arms race as 'Chain letters of Satan' is razor-sharp, while the chorus lines of 'a strange love is born' and 'Unholy union, trinity reformed' refer respectively to the 1964 anti-nuclear satirical film *Dr Strangelove* and the site in New Mexico where the first atomic bomb was detonated – codenamed 'Trinity'. The somewhat odd 'E=mc2 you can relate' comes from the fact that Einstein was persuaded to lend his name to an appeal to the US government before the outbreak of the Second World War to prioritise a nuclear weapons development programme. It was feared that the Nazi powers may already be heading down that path, and the irony here is that far from this being the case, even when hearing of the US nuclear plans, Hitler and his aides dismissed it as propaganda. Few realise today how influential Einstein inadvertently was on the dawn of the nuclear age.

The line 'Whatever would Robert have said to his God?' is almost certainly double-edged. The Robert in question is, of course, Robert Oppenheimer, known as the 'father of the atomic bomb', but the exact phrasing probably also nods to the song 'Whatever Would Robert Have Said' by Van der Graaf Generator. This band were admired by Steve Harris in particular – although in that case, the Robert alluded to is Robert Van der Graff (note the different spelling), inventor of the generator in question.

So, this lengthy song is a lyrical triumph without doubt, but what of the music? That's a difficult one, as it really is nothing like a typical Maiden-style song. The riff driving the verses is mid-paced and crushingly heavy, rather akin to Metallica circa their *And Justice for All* album, and the predominant guitar in the first verse fights for space a little against the vocals, giving a slightly jarring effect. The chorus is a little more Maiden-esque, while the fast verses mid-song also clatter along reassuringly. However, some of the changes from one section to another feel clumsy and ill-thought-out, such as the end of the chorus, for example. However, repeated listens do appease these reservations somewhat and, while it isn't the sharpest or most effective musical piece on the album, its progressive leanings should be applauded. The days of even *The Number of the Beast* seem quite basic in comparison now. The solos are by Smith first, and then Gers a couple of minutes later.

'The Pilgrim' (Gers, Harris)

The opening to this track features a stately, Arabic-sounding guitar figure which takes us straight back to 'The Nomad', and bodes well for another stirring epic. Disappointingly, this turns on a dime almost straight away to become a rather generic Maiden rocker. These Arabic echoes return to lift things periodically, notably after the choruses and during and after Janick's superb solo, and the opening bit returns briefly at the end, but it's all too many drab valleys thrown into relief by majestic peaks to work well. Lyrically it deals with setting out to new shores to deliver the word of God, whether through persuasive tongues or indeed sharp bladed weapons, and it would have been better served by different music. Initially, this was a contender to be the title of the album, but all in all, the song stands out as one which could easily have been dropped from the dogged plan to play the whole album. It's all right, but there are far better songs which have never been played live.

'The Longest Day' (Smith, Harris, Dickinson)

We're back on firm ground here with yet another gruelling Maiden saga of the Horrors of War, lest people should want to go around smiling recklessly while listening. Essentially, this is 'Paschendale' transplanted into the following war, as it deals with the Normandy beach landings in June 1944, a decisive moment which firmly turned the whole path of the conflict. Unlike the events in 'Paschendale', this was actually a triumphant victory which led directly to some good results, though like that earlier battle it did so at the cost of some significant human suffering, with men being mowed down as they ran for the beach from their landing craft, like a hellish shooting gallery – as mercilessly displayed during the opening 25-minutes of the film *Saving Private Ryan*.

The verses are punishingly heavy, with Dickinson spitting out the grimly visceral words with a horrible urgency, describing 'wretched souls puking, shaking fear, to take a bullet for those that sent them here', 'remorseless shrapnel', 'choking death', 'the rising dead, faces bloated, torn' and the water being 'red with the blood of the dead'. It doesn't pull any punches, and it works in tandem with the music – the verses and pre-chorus – quite brilliantly. Only the chorus, a repetitive refrain of 'How long on this longest day, 'til we finally make it through' lets things down somewhat, as it drops the intensity rather than escalating it. The instrumental section, however, illuminated by outstanding solos from Smith and then Murray, is outstanding, going through different moods, evoking the gunfire, the desperate trudge through the water and finally the victorious taking of the beach flawlessly. Unlike 'Brighter Than a Thousand Suns' the whole thing flows, and you can't see the join. One of the highlights of the album, the title is of course taken from the 1962 film of the same name, and the reference to Overlord in the lyric comes from Operation Overlord, the code name for the entire offensive.

Some light relief might be needed after this helping of grimly wrenching doom, but this is Iron Maiden delivering a conceptual album themed around war and destruction, so you definitely won't get it... or will you?

'Out of the Shadows' (Dickinson, Harris)
This rare example of an actual Iron Maiden 'power ballad' may not exactly be light, cheery fare, but it is nevertheless beautifully melodic and infused with a sense of hope, as it talks about reincarnation, and the pain in life being something which is necessary to be endured as new life and fresh happiness can emerge. All quiet verses and big stirring choruses, Dave Murray scatters six-string fairy dust throughout, especially during the verses as he exquisitely accompanies the stately vocal melody. Adrian Smith takes over for the actual 'solo' but doesn't let the side down as he too delivers a masterclass in controlled melodicism. This is a side of Maiden which could have been explored more often through their career, as they are very, very good at it when they want to be.

'The Reincarnation of Benjamin Breeg' (Murray, Harris)
Ah, put a hold on that lightness will you, because here comes the choking doom again, as we continue the rebirth theme with a guy who is the reincarnation of the sins of a thousand men, which is bound to put a crimp in your conscience, one would imagine. The song is narrated in the first person by Breeg, who craves the prospect of another reincarnation to end his current hell weighed down by the 'sin of a thousand souls'. It's another mid-paced anvil-heavy chugger, following the obligatory two-minute calm before the storm, and it's good at what it does. It's far from the most remarkable or catchy song on the album, however, which makes its choice as the lead-off single, released a couple of weeks before the album, utterly baffling. This is especially true considering that the combined length of the song and its B-side (a live 'Hallowed Be Thy Name') rendered it ineligible for consideration in the UK singles chart! The single had a nice cover by previous Maiden artist Melvyn Grant, featuring Eddie digging into Breeg's grave by moonlight with a pickaxe, with the tombstone reading 'Here lies a man about whom not much is known' in Hungarian.

Indeed, the conjecture partly arising from this hint reached epidemic debate among fans, and the appearance of a website purporting to be from an 'A Breeg', a relative of Benjamin, only stoked things further. In fact, this was planted by the band and mischievously included lots of supposed clues about his identity. This can all be found online, but one interesting thing is that the

121

website claims Breeg disappeared on 18 June 1978, which was shortly before the recording of *The Soundhouse Tapes* (18 June is also the date of Churchill's 'Finest Hour' speech, as used by the band), so it could be seen as Iron Maiden being a collective reincarnation of Breeg. But probably not.

There was a pressing error on the European version of the clear vinyl single which stated (like the US version) that it should be played at 33rpm, but it actually played at 45. At 33 as advised, it would have led to a very slow-paced song!

'For the Greater Good of God' (Harris)

Or, as it might as well be subtitled, 'You want epic? We'll give you epic!' – this nine-minute behemoth has the only genuine, dyed in the wool, air-punching chorus on the album. But it's worth waiting for. Lyrically, the song has a clear target – namely the rise of religious extremism and the death and war attributed to His name, and it's a well-structured lyric for sure, despite one or two slightly clumsy lines. It's certainly vintage Harris.

The track starts quietly yet again, only this time with a nice bass intro from Mr H, and this continues through the first part of the song proper. When the full band crash in for the remainder of the verse it is a little underwhelming, but fear not – here comes the mighty pre-chorus ('Please tell me now what love is', etc.) and the following chorus proper (you know what that's going to be – yep, the song title hammered home).

The instrumental section features all three guitarists getting a short solo – Janick first, then Smith and finally Murray – but the real gold peg you can hang your hat on here is that pre-chorus. Finish the verse, drop tempo a step, switch up an octave and just listen to Bruce go! Marvellous stuff. Might just be the best song on the album.

'Lord of Light' (Smith, Harris, Dickinson)

Well, with all of this grim suffering and destruction happening, you might as well all start worshipping Satan, Bruce seems to be advising us here, as it is, of course, he who is the 'Lord of Light'. Kind of drastic, Bruce, but do go on...

In effect, there has been so much bad stuff going on that the alternative, the Lord of Light fallen angel Lucifer himself, might as well be given a crack, is the implication here. The lyric looks at the situation from the point of view of Lucifer as a 'fallen angel', rather than a 'devil', and it certainly has some interesting imagery without being the most memorable. This goes for the music as well, which has a nice sinister opening (quiet intro again, as per the template, of course) followed by an arresting moment when the band crash in with all the force of, well, an angel falling to earth. This soon dissipates, however, and neither the verse or chorus have much in the way of memorable or distinctive melodies. Smith and Murray solo away in determined fashion toward the end, but without really lifting proceedings.

This is the point where things started to really outstay their welcome during the live shows as the audience, having had an hour of new music coming to a stirring peak with 'For the Greater Good of God', began noticeably shifting in their seats and looking at their watches a little. The momentum of the show was compromised at this exact point to my eyes.

'The Legacy' (Gers, Harris)

And so, we arrive at another nine-minute epic to close the album on what certainly counts as a high note, if arguably not the highest. Lyrically this is in three parts, with the first dealing with some men 'dressed in black' sent to war but coming back with their minds altered by a 'strange yellow gas', which seems to have been administered as some sort of experiment by their own commanding forces. This is revealed in the second part, where we see a world leader of indeterminate origin on his death bed being unmasked as a fraud, speaking of peace but sending his men to an unspecified fate and the world to the brink of disaster. This has often been linked with the 1990 film *Jacob's Ladder*, with its similar tale of long-term nightmares and delusion brought about by an experimental gas, but any connection or inspiration is purely conjecture. The third lyrical theme moves things onto a world stage with the hope that man can work together to bring us back from the precipice to which we have been led.

It's meaty stuff for sure, and for the most part, the music matches up. The first three minutes are pure progressive rock, as the end of the trademark acoustic opening only leads us to a new instrumental section driven by acoustic guitars but interrupted by regular outbursts of power chording, as if the band are trying to break through. It's superb, and when the 'big riffing' finally enters at just past the three-minute mark, it seems perfect. There is no chorus here, but the verse thunders along with the propulsive, 'epic' nature of prime early Rainbow, before a fast riff straight from Black Sabbath's self-titled song ushers in an instrumental section featuring an excellent Janick solo. If the song had ended at this point, it would be a solid contender for album peak, but things drift off a little as a new musical development arrives for the climactic lyrical section. It clearly seeks to add dramatic impetus to the worldwide focus of this final part, but somehow it does the opposite and just plods on until brief reprises of earlier themes bring things to a close. It's frustrating, as a really big anthemic ending would have launched this to the pantheon of genuine Maiden classics.

A strong closer still, however, to an album which is certainly strong, if not as strong as the band clearly felt it to be, and one whose reputation was sadly forever tarnished for some fans who reacted badly to the shows.

Related songs:
'Hocus Pocus' (Van Leer)

Only one entry to report on here, with this Focus cover featured on the DVD single version of 'Different World'. All other single B-sides and additional tracks were live versions of earlier Maiden tracks. This version is well played

123

but ultimately pointless. The riff is tailor-made for Maiden, but with Nicko taking over the original Thijs Van Leer vocal interjections in self-consciously 'wacky' style, it soon outstays its welcome. It's clear that the band had a good time doing it, and obviously, it's not to be taken entirely seriously, but really it doesn't accomplish anything. Essentially, the good bits are good because they sound like the original, the bad bits are bad because they don't.

The Final Frontier

Personnel:
Bruce Dickinson: vocals
Dave Murray: guitars
Janick Gers: guitars
Adrian Smith: guitars
Steve Harris: bass guitar, keyboards
Nicko McBrain: drums
Record Label: EMI (UK), UME/Sony (US)
Recorded: Jan-Feb 2010, produced by Kevin Shirley and Steve Harris
Release date: 13 August 2010
Highest chart places: UK: 1, USA: 4
Running time: 76:34

Four years on from the last album, this represented the longest gap between albums of the band's career – though that would be broken by the next release. It was also the longest album of the band's career up to this point – something which would *also* be broken by the next one! Convening in January 2010, the band returned to Compass Point in the Bahamas for the first time since 'Somewhere in Time' almost 25 years earlier. Bruce Dickinson commented on the fact that the place remained 'spookily' unchanged since they had last been there, but that these familiar surroundings helped them relax and eased the recording process.

For the first time there were no single releases from the album, with the nearest being three songs ('El Dorado', 'Satellite 15' and 'Coming Home') released as radio promos with 'single edits'. By this time the single format was largely an irrelevance in the rock world, so this is perhaps not surprising. Who knows, the 76-minute duration might have been less, had there been an outlet for one or two tracks to be released away from the album itself. On the other hand, probably not, since new original songs used as B-sides had not been a feature for quite some time – if we discount the vacuous jams, that is. Interestingly, Steve Harris received a writing credit on every song, though only one solo credit. Adrian Smith explained this at the time by remarking that Harris had become more interested in writing lyrics and finishing touches to songs, as well as arrangements, as opposed to doing too much writing on his own.

Touring the album, the band distanced themselves from the 'new material overkill' approach, with just five of the album's ten tracks being played in the set. Of course, this was still over 40 minutes of new material, which amounted to an album in the vinyl days, but spread out through the set it made for a much more well-received show in most quarters.

Album Cover:

Melvyn Grant was back for the album's cover, which looked a little more typically 'Maiden' than the previous two, but still received its share of criticism.

It featured Eddie as a strange alien creature appearing to be brandishing some sort of glowing key for no particular purpose, as he breaks into a space helmet containing an alien skeletal head. It's certainly a little on the dark side, both in mood and colour, but what seemed to agitate many fans was the argument that the creature might not even be Eddie, this making it the first-ever Maiden cover without his presence. Leaving aside the whole other argument about whether the band had boxed themselves into a bit of a creative corner with the mandatory Eddie cover by now, it does seem clear that the alien is too similar in an intentionally otherworldly format not to represent him. The inside and back covers of the CD were utterly uninspiring unless a silhouetted band photo and a bit of a planet happen to get one's creative juices flowing, while the booklet contained the usual lyrics and backdrop images, though in fairness there are a couple of very nice images once one gets past the inevitable aliens. All in, it's a little dull.

The three radio promo 'singles' came with interesting cover art by Anthony Dry, however, as mocked-up comic-strip panels numbered as issues '15', '15A' and '15B', being the three 'singles' from album fifteen. A shame these images weren't more widely seen – their use in the album cover design would have certainly brightened proceedings.

'Satellite 15... The Final Frontier' (Smith, Harris)
Essentially, this opener is two distinct tracks welded together to make a single eight-minute whole, though quite why is unclear. The 'Satellite 15' portion is a fascinating space-rock collage of tribal-sounding hypnotic drums and slashing, claustrophobic power-chords. The vocals enter, beginning the tale of an astronaut lost in space who is going to drift to his death, but the vocal gets somewhat lost in this first section.

Around halfway through a typical Maiden heavy riff enters to herald the 'Final Frontier' section, wherein the doomed astronaut contemplates his fate – complete with a nice reference to Icarus. A pair of brilliant solos, from Smith then Murray, lift the song up a level after the second chorus, before Smith comes in again as Dickinson declaims the final repetitive chorus. There was a video produced for this when it was released as a radio promo, but it consisted only of the second half of the track, as did the radio edit. Overall, it has to be said that indexing this as two separate tracks may have been a better option if they ran straight into each other anyway. A decent opening though, and the live-action *Star Wars*-cum-*Indiana Jones* video is excellent if nothing whatsoever to do with the lyric. It at least gets Alien Eddie in there though, and the mysterious key from the album cover as a bonus.

'El Dorado' (Smith, Harris, Dickinson)
This classic-style Maiden galloper bucks the usual trend of starting with a quiet intro by doing exactly the opposite – opening with a big crescendo, in the vein of Deep Purple's 'Speed King' opening on the *In Rock* album. In truth, while

this is very much old-school stuff, it is also one of the weaker tracks on the album. Telling the story of a conman offering to take people to the fabled 'city of gold' Eldorado, it just doesn't have enough to set it apart from the pack. The verses hurtle along pleasantly enough on a propulsive bass-driven riff, but the pre-chorus is very weak and lets the side down somewhat. The main chorus is a little stronger, and Smith / Murray / Gers give us a nice enough three-part solo, in that order, but overall it just feels a bit too generic, 'Maiden by numbers' to stand out. It has been suggested that the lyric is an extended metaphor for politicians promising things they can't deliver with lies, but there is no direct evidence for this, so it may simply be a tale used to illustrate the legend.

There are a couple of lines of note in the lyric. The first is 'I'm the jester with no tears', which seems perhaps too close to Marillion's 'Script for a Jester's Tear' not to be a tip of the hat, while the line 'I'm a clever banker's face, with just a letter out of place' comes from the English 'rhyming slang' use of the word 'Banker' – or 'Merchant Banker' – to mean 'wanker', which is what Bruce is saying here.

'Mother of Mercy' (Smith, Harris)
Don't be too shocked, but this song has Steve Harris writing about a soldier on a battlefield. Yes, it's getting a little past cliché by now, but to be fair this is one of his stronger lyrics, with religion being very much the focal point and the seeming cause of the conflict in which the protagonist finds himself. It's effective at setting the scene of the unpleasantness and ugliness of the battle, but he has had some practice at that by now! Musically it's pretty good, a quiet, but not typically slow, intro building up gradually to explode into some staccato riffing before we begin the more usual Maiden giddy-up. Smith supplies the solo, as he often does in his own songs, and it's a good one. The protagonist of the song rejects the religion and false teachings which caused him to be in this situation, but he seems to hold some faith still as he appeals to the unspecified 'Mother of Mercy' in the chorus.

It has to be noted that there are a couple of rather glaringly clumsy lines in the song, grammatically speaking, probably caused by a syllable being needed. 'I'm at a place of where I give no grace' seems to be tying itself in knots a little, but the biggest offender is the awkward extra 'of' in 'I'll die a lonely death, of that I'm certain of', which rivals Paul McCartney's infamous 'ever-changing world in which we live in' from 'Live and Let Die'! It does seem quite odd for Harris to do this, as he is certainly a very literate and well-read lyricist, so perhaps we should let it pass...

'Coming Home' (Smith, Harris, Dickinson)
This is another of those Maiden 'power ballads', and one of the very best of them all. This magnificently stirring and evocative song is Dickinson articulating how it feels to be flying the Maiden plane Ed Force One back to England ('to Albion's land'), and home again. His descriptive imagery here

is nothing short of brilliant ('Curving on the edge of daylight 'til it slips into the void', 'Stretched the fingers of my hand, covered countries with my span', 'Flown the dark Atlantic over Mariners' stormy graves'), while the chorus with its descriptions of coming in to land, with 'when I see the runway lights in the misty dawn' and 'as the vapour trails alight' is so emotionally charged, musically, that it could easily induce tears in someone the least bit homesick. Not a note is wasted here, there are no power chords or galloping basslines for the sake of it, and the result is the best song on the album without a doubt – to these ears at least. Murray and then Smith both provide solos of admirable taste, restraint and feeling.

This is the sort of track that most people don't even realise Iron Maiden can do. Which is an enormous shame, as this is an example which can stand with any you might care to name. The band clearly felt the same as, despite not being an obvious 'live' song, it was played on every date of the following tour. Great job guys, great job.

'The Alchemist' (Gers, Harris, Dickinson)

Normal service is resumed here with this fast rocker, but it's a very good one, delivered at a higher tempo than the stereotypical Maiden 'charge'. The bulk of the music is by Gers, but the scholarly lyrics are again from Dickinson. For this one, he out-histories the master Harris as he delves into the life of a man many won't even be aware of: Elizabethan mathematician, astrologer and occult philosopher John Dee. Credited with coining the term 'British Empire' for the first time, he was in the trusted service of Queen Elizabeth I (the 'frozen queen' in the lyric), but he moved to the continent and fell in with a man named Edward Kelley (misspelt in the lyric as 'Kelly'), an occultist and generally accepted charlatan. He began to exert enormous influence over Dee, claiming to have spoken with angels in the Enochian language, which some believe he invented, until finally causing a falling out when he managed to convince Dee that the spirits had commanded that they share his wife! Despite the fact that, at that time, Dee was 60 and Kelley 52, she fell pregnant by one of them, which is an impressive feat in biological terms. Dee returned home to find his home at Mortlake had been vandalised and most of his vast library of books stolen or destroyed. He lived to the age of 81, remarkable for the time, but sadly ended his life in poverty, having to sell off his prized possessions. The lyric does a tremendous job of alluding to all of the salient points and is unusual for a song so fast and relatively simple. Gers himself contributes the solo, and all in all, it is an excellent track once again.

'Isle of Avalon' (Smith, Harris)

Time for another epic now, with this nine-minute trip through a cornucopia of Celtic mythical imagery, which seems to be appealing to the 'earth goddess', or Mother Nature, to fight back against the neglect she has suffered at the hands of modern men. All manner of things collide in this opaque yet fascinating lyric, from pagan rituals (corn dolls and the like) through to the myths surrounding the legendary Isle of Avalon. Musically, it is good without being remarkable, as it tends to drift by well enough without too much that is memorable going on. The exception to that is the instrumental section, which is remarkable; Dave Murray's superb guitar solo leads into a section full of prog-metal riffing, reminiscent of Rush, while Adrian Smith pulls out one of his finest solos in terms of complementing the accompaniment. It's not in the top echelon of Maiden epics, but there are a lot worse.

'Starblind' (Smith, Harris, Dickinson)
In the pantheon of overlooked and misunderstood Iron Maiden songs, this one ranks pretty highly. Often criticised in reviews of the album, and rarely singled out for praise in fan discussions, it is In fact a superb track which reveals its secrets slowly on repeated listening. What at first can appear to be low on hooks, big themes and choruses, emerges with familiarity to be extremely well constructed, with parts that will eventually, when the time is right, lodge themselves in your brain and set up home there. There is more prog than metal here, huge Sabbath-style distorted guitar riffs notwithstanding. Lyrically also, one could spend a year studying these words and still not grasp everything which is being said. Once again by master wordsmith Dickinson (sorry Steve, but he is the greater man in terms of pen and paper), the main thrust dealing with organised religion, and the abuse of such power, with a recently deceased soul making its journey into the afterlife. There are nods to all manner of religious beliefs and images of the afterlife jostling for position here in a lyric which manages the balancing act between opaqueness and curiosity to perfection.

Adrian Smith – who seems quite adept when it comes to epics now after his late start on them – takes almost all of the solos and provides the guitar interjections scattered around this song like, well, stardust. Dave Murray comes in with one brief flurry shortly before the five-minute mark, but blink and you'd miss it.

Musically and lyrically, within the parameters of Iron Maiden's chosen musical habitat, it is hard to imagine getting much further from 'Running Free' than this. Well, until the next album, but we'll come to that!

'The Talisman' (Gers, Harris)
Nine minutes again, so yet another multi-faceted epic then? Well, no, not really. This tale of seafarers seeking a new land, but enduring a terrible crossing starts well enough for sure, with an atmospheric scene-setting opening played out for almost two-and-a-half minutes, which is similar to 'The Legacy' on the previous album. The band now hurtle in with a truly thrilling riff which sounds just for a second as if the mainsail on the ship has come crashing down around us. Unfortunately, that thrilling riff is mostly what you'll get for the next six-and-a-half minutes, by which time it's notably less thrilling. This is, in effect, a

decent five-minute rocker stretched out beyond breaking point and given a hat with 'Epic' written on it. And what exactly is the mysterious talisman the guy has clutched in his hand, which they are apparently 'sailing by'? There seems to be no clue given and, like the music, this promising lyrical idea runs out of steam after a while, and the song comes to a somewhat anticlimactic end. Janick handles the solo in this one, as one might expect as it's largely his song.

'The Man Who Would Be King' (Gers, Harris)
A nice short one now, as this is only eight-and-a-half minutes, practically The Ramones by Maiden standards by this point! I speak in jest of course, but these lengthy pieces are beginning to need a bit of leavening by now. First off here, it's that intro again, quiet, reflective, blah blah. Two-and-a-half minutes and in crash the band, and away we go into 'the gallop'. The instrumental mid-song, after Murray's unspectacular solo, is superb, but all too soon it's back down to the really rather run-of-the-mill riff. Even the band sound a bit disinterested playing this. The confusing lyrics don't really help, talking about someone who seems to be running from a crime, though oddly doing so on a donkey. The crime may be justified or self-defence, but we don't really care as the biblical clichés pile up, as does the announcement that he 'would be king', though why and of what we are not told. They were padding filler out to enormous lengths by this point, when the album would actually be stronger for a little pruning, and this – probably the weakest song on here – only exemplifies that. Hopefully, the last track on the album can arrest the mini-slide...

'When the Wild Wind Blows' (Harris)
A full eleven minutes here for this grand finale to the album, and this time there is no misstep: this is an epic on the grand Maiden scale, and a good one. The inspiration for the song is the book of the same name by Raymond Briggs, a graphic novel telling the moving and allegorical tale of an ordinary couple who hear there is likely to be a nuclear catastrophe and he prepares a shelter while she goes about her normal days' routine, preparing tea and the like. After the bomb goes off, they emerge from the shelter and look back over their lives as they are irradiated. It's a grim tale, but one which Harris takes a step further: in this version of events, the TV announces that the threat has been called off, but after what turns out to be a minor earthquake causes pictures to fall off the wall and the like they assume this is all lies and that the worst is coming. They are found dead later in the shelter, having taken poison rather than face the aftermath of the destruction which actually never came. It's a powerful ending, and arguably one which would have been better than the original, as Steve flexes his lyrical muscles, as if in response to Bruce's fine work on this album.

Musically this one matches up. It opens with a beautiful, slightly Celtic, lilting melody which begins with just guitar and vocal but is repeated with the full band. A heavier section at the time of the earthquake proves a bridge into a superb instrumental section, with Smith, Murray then Gers all getting a turn on the guitar solo carousel. This takes us into a magnificent closing section when the couple is denying the official word and preparing for the end, driven by a dark, menacing yet powerful riff and some of Dickinson's most unnervingly grim vocals. It's heavy stuff in more ways than one and leads into a final, spellbinding solo from Janick before a short reprise of the quiet introduction gives us the twist at the end, as they are found dead in each other's arms. Phew. The slight slump of the previous tracks is wiped away completely by this, perhaps the finest Harris solo song since 'Blood Brothers' (though 'For the Greater Good of God' could present an argument), and a close second to 'Coming Home' as the pick of this very, very strong album.

The Book of Souls
Personnel:
Bruce Dickinson: vocals, piano
Dave Murray: guitars
Janick Gers: guitars
Adrian Smith: guitars
Steve Harris: bass guitar, keyboards
Nicko McBrain: drums
Record Label: Parlophone (UK), Sanctuary/BMG (US)
Recorded: Sept-Dec 2014, produced by Kevin Shirley and Steve Harris
Release date: 4 September 2015
Highest chart places: UK: 1, USA: 4
Running time: 92:11

So here we are, at Iron Maiden's latest album at the time of writing, a big five years after the previous one, and just look at it! A sprawling double album containing three songs over ten minutes long, including one which reaches a full eighteen. They were making a statement of intent with this one, that much is for sure.

The recording sessions began in September 2014 in Guillaume Tell Studios, Paris – the first time the band had recorded there since *Brave New World*. The approach this time was markedly different from their usual time spent writing before entering the studio – on this occasion, they went in with only rough ideas, and wrote then recorded the songs as they went along, an approach which they claimed gave the album a spontaneity and live feel which it otherwise would have lacked. The release of the album was delayed until September 2015, and the tour until the beginning of the following year, because toward the end of recording a cancerous tumour was discovered at the back of Bruce Dickinson's tongue, which had to be treated aggressively before further band work was possible.

Songwriting-wise, this is a step back from the previous album, in the sense that Harris only has writing credits for six of the album's twelve songs, a fact which is partly explained by the fact that he had two bereavements during the sessions, one a family member and the other a close friend. Understandably, this disrupted his creative muse a little.

Thankfully, again at the time of writing, Dickinson's cancer is still leaving him alone, and he is back to firing on all cylinders. One other notable thing about the album is that it is the first in their career not to appear on EMI – both EMI and Sanctuary had been acquired by Warners, and the band moved to Parlophone in the UK.

Album Cover:
For the album cover, the band drafted in Mark Wilkinson, the prolific Marillion/ Fish cover artist who had previously worked with Maiden on *Live at Donington*

and the *Best of the 'B' Sides* compilation, as well as a couple of singles. The cover depicts Eddie as a character from Mayan history, or myth, which the band insisted suited the music owing to the Mayan culture having a rich tradition relating to souls. Maybe so, but the fact remains that the cover is rather a dull one, with the image dark on black and lacking colour. There was actually far better artwork used on a radio promo single and also a live 'tour sampler' album released shortly afterwards.

'If Eternity Should Fail' (Dickinson)

This eight-minute opener, in fact, wasn't even intended to be a Maiden song at all at first, as Dickinson had penned it for his upcoming solo album, and planned to have that as the album title as well – although it is still 'upcoming' as it has not yet appeared. By all accounts, Steve Harris heard it and immediately said 'We need that for Maiden', and so it was.

In fact, while it's a decent enough song, one gets the impression that it isn't quite as good as it would like to think it is. It begins with one of those trademarked 'moody quiet intros' for 90 seconds before the band enter with a curiously mid-paced tempo for an album opener. The lyrics are full of vague obfuscation, leading to theories popping up all over the place about the true meaning. It clearly seems to be talking about a world in which science and reason have gone so far that there is no place for the Old Gods any more, but with metaphorical elements about ships at the edge of a flat world closing down the sails.

It was much publicised at the time that this was the first-ever Maiden track to use 'Drop D' tuning, an old Black Sabbath staple which should make the music heavier, but somehow just doesn't. That said, the instrumental, with Adrian Smith taking all of the solos, is superlative and conspires to drag the whole track up a level.

Right at the end, we get a spoken word part from 'Necropolis', an immortal who is apparently 'The harvester of the soul meat', which it has to be said is a pretty cool job title! Other than that, his demonic appearance seems a little tacked on and unnecessary. It's a decent opener, but way short of the target it wants to hit.

'Speed of Light' (Smith, Dickinson)

Although it wasn't a true 'single' release, this track was released as a digital download ahead of the album (on 14 August), and also as a single-track CD, though the latter was exclusive to Best Buy in the US. With lyrics by Dickinson, it is a conglomeration of various astronomically-related themes, with the central thrust seeming to allude to going through a black hole and perishing (the references to plasma trails, event horizons and a 'hollow universe in space' pointing to this).

It's a catchy fast-paced rocker, not a Maiden classic but not really trying to be. As a relief from some of the heavy, earnest stuff on this album and as a one-off single release it does its job well, even if it does sound rather more like Judas Priest than Iron Maiden overall! Actually, on the subject of musical similarities, if you caught a Deep Purple nod at the beginning, you're not wrong. Dickinson said that when he heard the first riff, he thought it sounded 'like something off *Burn*' so, with the band all being big Purple fans, he decided to pull off an Ian Gillan-esque scream in homage. Yes, I'm sure he knows Gillan wasn't on *Burn*! Put your hand down at the back there. Once you know it's there, it is hard to ignore. The guitar solos are Murray followed by Smith.

There was a music video for the song, which mixed forty years of Maiden with forty years of video gaming, and it's brilliantly done, as Eddie battles through variants of games like *Donkey Kong*, *Duke Nukem*, and best of all 'The Number of the Beast' with the fight on the rocky ledge done as *Street Fighter*. In fact, after the video, a 'Speed of Light' game was released, in the old 8-bit format, as a free PC game which you could play via their website.

'The Great Unknown' (Smith, Harris)
With Harris providing lyrics this time out, this one appears to be about the subject of wars being motivated and started by greed – not an entirely unusual theme for him to draw inspiration from. Musically, it has to be said it doesn't hang together quite as well as the words do, with a grinding, heavy, slow-moving feel which is quite nice in itself, falling over as it fails to get married up to any particularly impressive vocal melodies. Dickinson sings much of the song in a high register which results in him audibly straining at times, though whether this had anything to do with his still-undiscovered illness remains unclear. He certainly isn't the silver-throated magician of 'Run to the Hills' on here, but then again, three-and-a-half decades can also account for that.

Janick takes the first solo here, over the Panzer-tank crushing inexorability of the first instrumental section, while Smith and Murray get in on the action a minute or so later.

'The Red and the Black' (Harris)
Thirteen minutes long, starting and ending with a bass solo – it's not too hard to guess at the composer of this one! Using the colours of a roulette wheel, and also playing cards, the song deals, by the look of it, with chance and fate. Musically, it's pretty impressive as well, but in a somewhat unusual way, as the song itself essentially finishes at around the seven-minute mark, seemingly a lesser moment on the album, before it then takes flight for a six-minute instrumental coda which raises the bar enormously, lifting it from a decent enough track to a great one. Smith, Gers then Murray trade solos before, a minute or so later, Smith takes another one himself and does so brilliantly. There is a moment midway through this section where the tempo suddenly kicks up a notch, and it is utterly thrilling. Disposable parts such as the 'where did that suddenly come from?' random chorus chant of 'oh-oh-oh' are forgotten as that glorious lengthy coda sweeps all before it.

The song has nothing whatsoever to do with the Blue Öyster Cult track of the same name, which has lyrics about the Canadian Mounted Police, of all things.

'When the River Runs Deep' (Smith, Harris)
Short, sharp shock time again – if the word 'short' means anything at this point, with this 'short song' running to some six minutes. Again, a decent enough track with some superb instrumental portions, it seems to be advising the listener to grasp any opportunity presented to them in life while they are still able to. Murray and Gers lock horns at the first soloing opportunity, before Smith takes a short solo himself, after a short break.

A nice track once again, without somehow being elevated to greatness.

'The Book of Souls' (Gers, Harris)
The first disc ends with this ten-minute monster from Gers and Harris, with Gers generally accepted to have come up with most of the music. The lyric tells of the rise and disastrous fall of the lost Mayan civilisation, and therefore ties in with the album cover, while the music gets all epic and 'Phrygian scale', at least for the first half of the track, which sees the guys in a 'Stargazer' kind of mood, by the sound of it. After the main body of the lyrics are done (that is to say, the conventional verses and choruses), the music kicks up to a faster tempo, with some hints of 'Losfer Words' in the riff, while Murray hits a brilliant solo. A little after this, Gers and then Smith also get praiseworthy turns in the limelight. It's a great epic Maiden piece, though not quite at the top of the tree – mainly due to the vocal melody which somehow doesn't possess quite the right gravitas that the subject material deserves. Good finish to Part One, though.

'Death or Glory' (Smith, Dickinson)
Back to familiar Dickinson lyrical ground here, with WWI fighter planes replacing the WWII model from 'Aces High'. This one is specifically about the legendary German ace Manfred von Richthofen, who once said of his red Fokker triplane that it could 'turn like a devil and climb like a monkey' – all referenced in the lyric. Musically, it's short and pretty safe, though the instrumental section with Murray and then Smith both on incendiary form in the solo department is magnificent. Good disc opener, but not quite a classic.

'Shadows of the Valley' (Gers, Harris)
Lyrically, this is a very biblical track, with the words making a great many references to the Bible, such as the killing of the firstborn, the Commandments, 'though I walk in the valley of the shadow of death', etc., while the old man who 'lived a time and a half' must refer to the long-lived Moses, with 'the script of the book that he wrote' being the first five books of the Old Testament, which are credited to him. It seems to deal mainly with the vague concepts of sin (Original and 'regular') and damnation/

redemption. Musically we are on familiar ground, with what starts out as just another sprightly fast rocker with some nice intro bits once again turning into something much better with the instrumental section and stellar solos by Gers, Smith then Murray. It is becoming notable by this time that, while this album may lack a little of the great songwriting of some of its forebears, the quality of the solos by all three men has rarely been surpassed.

'Tears of a Clown' (Smith, Harris)
I know. You see the title and your brain immediately locates Smokey Robinson. It's unavoidable. This song has very little in common musically with that one, however, that's for sure, as this cruises by beautifully on a mid-paced, loping riff with just the right amount of crunch in the guitars. The song was inspired by the tragic suicide of comedian Robin Williams, and Harris here delivers his tribute to the man while looking behind the smile at the demons he was facing. It's actually a great song, and all the better for not trying to be anything more than it is – which does afflict some tracks on the album to an extent. The chorus is among the strongest on the record, and with Smith and Murray delivering a couple of their very best ever solos it's an often-overlooked gem and a real triumph. Indeed, Dickinson himself has called it his favourite on the album, which is easy to understand for a singer, with the vocal melodies being so good.

'The Man of Sorrows' (Murray, Harris)
From the title, it might initially appear that we are following up the previous song's inspiration, but close inspection of the lyric suggests that there might very well be some spill-over from the real-life tragedies Harris was witnessing at the time of recording, as it almost sounds like a thinly disguised cry for help. Musically, this is a rather frustrating track as it starts brilliantly but fails to keep it up. The opening, with Murray's beautiful guitar work skittering across the plangent guitar backing, is magnificent, as is Bruce's affecting delivery of the first verse. However, when the full band enter, rather than boosting the sound and kicking the song on, the opposite seems to happen with the song gradually losing all of its momentum as it struggles to raise much in the way of enthusiasm. The mid-section solos by MSG (Murray, Smith, Gers – not Michael Schenker Group or monosodium glutamate!) are themselves curiously muted affairs, and the song really has nowhere to go.

Note that Dickinson also had a solo song called 'Man of Sorrows' – no definite article, you will notice – on his 1997 album *Accident of Birth*, but there is no connection to this one at all.

'Empire of the Clouds' (Dickinson)
The only solo Dickinson song on the album – but that's somewhat made up for by the very fact that it lasts a whopping eighteen minutes! It's probably safe to say that, whatever people were expecting with the album, this wasn't it. And

yet, not only does it work but it does so triumphantly.

The subject matter of the song is the R101 airship, which famously crashed in France on 5 October 1930, on its maiden overseas flight, en route to India. The lyrics are extremely detailed and accurate in terms of the disaster. Full speed trials had not been carried out, yet the Certificate of Airworthiness was awarded nonetheless, water ballast was indeed jettisoned as the song describes and the politician referred to is probably Lord Thomson, Secretary of State for Air, who was killed in the crash. Altogether, 48 of the 54 people on board lost their lives. Even the line about 'experienced men asleep in their graves' has its roots in fact, as at least one crew member, Chief Electrician Arthur Disley, was dozing in the switch room when he was roused to try in vain to help prevent the disaster.

When he began composing the song, Dickinson had just completed the lyric to 'Death or Glory' and, having some air-related words unused, decided to write another song about the R101, a subject in which he has a keen interest. The song soon outgrew its relatively minor 'parent' to become arguably the masterpiece of the album. The music was composed by Dickinson on the Steinway grand piano in the studios, and according to the rest of the band, he spent a significant amount of time working alone on the song in a soundproof booth with the piano. On the final recording, he played the whole thing on the piano and recorded vocals, so the rest of the band had to play their parts along to the Dickinson piano recording, which is an astonishing thing for a man who had never played keyboards on an album previously. There was also orchestration added to the finished track, arranged by Jeff Bova.

The first ten minutes or so is a gradual build-up from the sparse piano opening through to the full weight of the band, and it does build very organically rather than falling into the latter-day Maiden trap of 'quiet intro then, bang, in we go, lads!' After the verse ending with 'Now she slips into our past' at around the seven-minute mark, an instrumental section begins which lasts for around eight minutes, conjuring up everything from the triumphant take-off and soaring into the air, accompanied by strident guitar work, mostly from Adrian Smith, through the technical problems and battling against them before coming to a head as everything begins to go wrong in chaos, at which point the vocals re-enter, and the song approaches its climax. It's brilliantly structured, with the long instrumental section continuing the theme of the vocal opening, rendering the whole piece akin to a movie for your ears, as it has been described. Dave Murray takes a solo at around the ten-minute mark, but the clear star here is Adrian Smith's solo at twelve minutes or so, which is spectacular. The final closure to the song, paying tribute to the dead, is very moving, and overall the piece is an astonishing compositional work by Dickinson. It has been suggested by many that this may well be Iron Maiden's recorded swansong, and if that does turn out to be true then 'Empire of the Clouds' would be a fitting curtain call.

The debut album began with the three minutes and 56 seconds of 'Prowler'.

There can scarcely be a greater contrast between that rudimentary if exciting work and 'Empire of the Clouds' – indeed, 'Empire' clocks in at around half the length of the entire Maiden debut album! Perhaps the greatest achievement of Iron Maiden, and by extension Steve Harris, whose musical taste the band has always so closely mirrored, is that they remain firmly fixed with a particular image and sound imprinted on the public consciousness while still producing works like this one. This track, 'Ancient Mariner', 'Blood Brothers' and the like take their vast army of fans on a musical journey way beyond that stereotype. That's a neat balancing act if you can pull it off, which the band have been doing ever since they put out 'Hallowed Be Thy Name' back in 1982.

Live Albums, Videos and Compilations
Live Albums
There have been masses of Iron Maiden live recordings through the years, but it was not ever thus. As with a lot of bands, the CD age and easier to use and better live recording technology, brought a flurry of live albums.

Not counting the *Live + One* EP, released in Japan in 1980, or indeed the *Maiden Japan* EP either, the first official live album came in 1985 with the seminal *Live After Death*. It sports a classic Riggs cover featuring Eddie bursting out of a grave (accompanied by an obligatory Edgar Allan Poe quote), which reads 'Edward T. H...'. It is implied that the obscured word is 'Head', making the name 'Eddie The 'Ead'. The album has become regarded as a classic. Recorded on the 1984 World Slavery tour, it is nevertheless evenly spread with songs from *Powerslave* (four), *Piece of Mind* (four) and *The Number of the Beast* (five). The first two albums chip in with three and one respectively. Many of these renditions have become arguably regarded as definitive, and it is an album which should reside in any serious rock fan's collection.

Following this, was an eight-year live drought before the album *A Real Live One* was released in March 1993. Recorded in 1992, and again having nice Riggs artwork, the album featured only material from *Somewhere in Time* onward (that is to say, beyond the scope of *Live After Death*). A companion album arrived in October, however, entitled *A Real Dead One*, and this time contained only material from *Powerslave* and before. Proving that, like buses, live albums often make you wait for ages before several come at once, this was followed almost immediately, in November 1993, with the album *Live at Donington 1992*. It was released on triple vinyl and double CD and unsurprisingly finds the band captured live at the Donington festival, which was notable as the show which saw Adrian Smith join them on guitar for 'Running Free'.

In 1994 an album called *Maiden England* appeared, recorded in Birmingham in 1988, though this took the format of a CD included with a VHS or DVD. It did receive a full-show CD release some years later, renamed *Maiden England '88*. 2002 saw a much more significant release, with *Rock in Rio*, recorded at that huge festival in Brazil, coming out. Recorded during the *Brave New World* tour, the album contains six tracks out of nineteen from the band's then-current album. It is also notable for definitive performances of the Blaze-era songs 'Sign of the Cross' and 'The Clansman'. After this, the floodgates opened somewhat and new releases such as the box set *Eddie's Archive* appeared late the same year, and *Death on the Road*, commemorating the *Dance of Death* tour, arrived in 2005. 2009 brought us *Flight 666* in May, the soundtrack to the documentary film. *En Vivo* in 2012 and *Book of Souls: The Live Chapter* were straightforward live albums from *The Final Frontier* and *Book of Souls* tours.

Compilations
Once again, there was very little until we get to the '90s and then it's a case of 'Good Lord, make them stop'. The first Maiden compilation was *Best of*

the Beast, which was released in both single CD and two-CD editions. 2002 brought *Edward the Great: Their Greatest Hits*, while *Best of the 'B' Sides* ended up as a disc in the *Eddie's Archive* box. The heroically inventively titled *The Essential Iron Maiden* came to fruition in 2005 also, spread across two discs. Finally, in 2008, we got *Somewhere Back in Time: The Best of 1980-1989*, which did what it said on the tin, albeit only with a single disc. It tied in with the similarly-named tour playing the old songs.

DVD and Video

The band have actually been well served by the visual medium, with a dizzying array of titles appearing over the years. The very first of these was *Live at the Rainbow* in 1981, containing seven tracks featuring the *Killers* line-up. A couple of Sony 'Video EPs' followed, with *Video Pieces* in 1983 containing four promo videos, and *Behind the Iron Curtain* in 1985 with four live tracks filmed in Eastern Europe. Slim pickings on both of those.

The *Live After Death* album also appeared on video, which contained the Long Beach material which formed the first three sides of the album (albeit filmed on a different night). It, therefore, omitted the tracks from the fourth vinyl side which was from Hammersmith but did include an encore of 'Sanctuary' which was absent from the album. The later DVD release contained a second disc full of extras, including an expanded version of *Behind the Iron Curtain* with three extra songs and also a film of the band supporting Queen at Rock in Rio 1985.

Next up in 1987 came *Twelve Wasted Years*, a documentary covering the band's history from 1975-'87, with archive footage of fourteen songs, while 1989 brought us the celebrated *Maiden England*, consisting of superb material filmed in Birmingham on the Seventh Tour of a Seventh Tour. It is now available on DVD and double CD under the title *Maiden England '88* featuring a lot more material than the original VHS release. At this point, you might have wanted a break in order to catch up with watching all of these, but no such luck as *The First Ten Years* in 1989 gave us 21 promo videos from the band's career thus far. After the *Live at Donington* album in its video incarnation, we then got *Raising Hell* in 1994, which was yet more live footage, this time from Pinewood Studios in London. The band appeared together with a 'horror magician' named Simon Drake, who ran amok with a series of Alice Cooper-type tricks, including amputating Dave Murray's hands and 'killing' Bruce Dickinson and a large number of the audience and crew. Quite...

Thankfully there was now a break from this constant barrage until 2001, when a *Classic Albums* look at *The Number of the Beast* led into the superb *Rock in Rio* DVD the following year. Don't get too relaxed, however, as 2003 brought us a double DVD entitled *Visions of the Beast*, which was an updated look at every promo video to date. That's forty of the damn things! There's no break, though, as 2004 documentary *The Early Days* led into 2006 and *Death on the Road*, filmed on – well, you know which tour. Some of these are starting to look a little samey by now. The concert documentary film *Flight 666* in 2009 was a little different, and very enjoyable, but there was a sense of inevitability about the double DVD release *En Vivo* (2012), recorded on *The Final Frontier* tour. Surprisingly, this format was not followed up for *Book of Souls: The Live Chapter*, which had a video version available for paid download but no plans for a physical release. Sign of the times really, one supposes. A long way from the VHS of *Live at the Rainbow*, but once again perfectly encapsulating the astonishing longevity of this metal institution.

Up The Irons!

Afterword: 30 Numbers of the Beast – Author's Maiden Playlist

Remember Tomorrow
Wrathchild
The Number of the Beast
Run to the Hills
Hallowed Be Thy Name
Where Eagles Dare
Revelations
The Trooper
Powerslave
The Rime of the Ancient Mariner
Wasted Years
Infinite Dreams
Holy Smoke
Afraid to Shoot Strangers
Judas Be My Guide

Fear of the Dark
Fortunes of War
Judgement of Heaven
Judgement Day
Ghost of the Navigator
Brave New World
Blood Brothers
Nomad
Paschendale
Face in the Sand
For the Greater Good of God
Coming Home
Where the Wild Wind Blows
Tears of a Clown
Empire of the Clouds

Bibliography:

Dickinson, B., *What Does This Button Do?* (Harper Collins, 2017)

Shooman, J., *Bruce Dickinson: Maiden Voyage, The Biography* (Music Press, 2016)

Juras, S., *Steve Harris: The Clairvoyant* (Scott Butler, 2013, 2002)

Wall, M., *Last of the Giants: The Iron Maiden Biography* (Orion, 2017)

Popoff, M., *Iron Maiden Album by Album* (Voyageur, 2018)

Daniels, N., *The Ultimate Illustrated History of the Beast* (Voyageur, 2016)

Popoff, M., *Wheels of Steel: The Explosive Early Years of NWOBHM* (Wymer, 2019)

Dickinson, B., *The Adventures of Lord Iffy Boatrace* (Sidgewick & Jackson, 1990)

Dickinson, B., *The Missionary Position: The Further Advances of Lord Iffy Boatrace* (Sidgewick & Jackson, 1992)

On Track series
Queen – Andrew Wild 978-1-78952-003-3
Emerson Lake and Palmer – Mike Goode 978-1-78952-000-2
Deep Purple and Rainbow 1968-79 – Steve Pilkington 978-1-78952-002-6
Yes – Stephen Lambe 978-1-78952-001-9
Blue Oyster Cult – Jacob Holm-Lupo 978-1-78952-007-1
The Beatles – Andrew Wild 978-1-78952-009-5
Roy Wood and the Move – James R Turner 978-1-78952-008-8
Genesis – Stuart MacFarlane 978-1-78952-005-7
JethroTull – Jordan Blum 978-1-78952-016-3
The Rolling Stones 1963-80 – Steve Pilkington 978-1-78952-017-0
Judas Priest – John Tucker 978-1-78952-018-7
Toto – Jacob Holm-Lupo 978-1-78952-019-4
Van Der Graaf Generator – Dan Coffey 978-1-78952-031-6
Frank Zappa 1966 to 1979 – Eric Benac 978-1-78952-033-0
Elton John in the 1970s – Peter Kearns 978-1-78952-034-7
The Moody Blues – Geoffrey Feakes 978-1-78952-042-2
The Beatles Solo 1969-1980 – Andrew Wild 978-1-78952-030-9
Steely Dan – Jez Rowden 978-1-78952-043-9
Hawkwind – Duncan Harris 978-1-78952-052-1
Fairport Convention – Kevan Furbank 978-1-78952-051-4
Iron Maiden – Steve Pilkington 978-1-78952-061-3
Dream Theater – Jordan Blum 978-1-78952-050-7
10CC – Peter Kearns 978-1-78952-054-5
Gentle Giant – Gary Steel 978-1-78952-058-3
Kansas – Kevin Cummings 978-1-78952-057-6
Mike Oldfield – Ryan Yard 978-1-78952-060-6
The Who – Geoffrey Feakes 978-1-78952-076-7

On Screen series
Carry On... – Stephen Lambe 978-1-78952-004-0
Powell and Pressburger – Sam Proctor 978-1-78952-013-2
Seinfeld Seasons 1 to 5 – Stephen Lambe 978-1-78952-012-5
Francis Ford Coppola – Cam Cobb and Stephen Lambe 978-1-78952-022-4
Monty Python – Steve Pilkington 978-1-78952-047-7
Doctor Who: The David Tennant Years – Jamie Hailstone 978-1-78952-066-8
James Bond – Andrew Wild 978-1-78952-010-1

Other Books
Not As Good As The Book – Andy Tillison 978-1-78952-021-7
The Voice. Frank Sinatra in the 1940s – Stephen Lambe 978-1-78952-032-3
Maximum Darkness – Deke Leonard 978-1-78952-048-4
The Twang Dynasty – Deke Leonard 978-1-78952-049-1
Maybe I Should've Stayed In Bed – Deke Leonard 978-1-78952-053-8
Tommy Bolin: In and Out of Deep Purple – Laura Shenton 978-1-78952-070-5
Jon Anderson and the Warriors - the road to Yes – David Watkinson
978-1-78952-059-0

and many more to come!

Would you like to write for Sonicbond Publishing?

At Sonicbond Publishing we are always on the look-out for authors, particularly for our two main series:

On Track. Mixing fact with in depth analysis, the On Track series examines the work of a particular musical artist or group. All genres are considered from easy listening and jazz to 60s soul to 90s pop, via rock and metal.

On Screen. This series looks at the world of film and television. Subjects considered include directors, actors and writers, as well as entire television and film series. As with the On Track series, we balance fact with analysis.

While professional writing experience would, of course, be an advantage the most important qualification is to have real enthusiasm and knowledge of your subject. First-time authors are welcomed, but the ability to write well in English is essential.

Sonicbond Publishing has distribution throughout Europe and North America, and all books are also published in E-book form. Authors will be paid a royalty based on sales of their book.

Further details are available from www.sonicbondpublishing.co.uk. To contact us, complete the contact form there or email info@sonicbondpublishing.co.uk